The Pure Land Handbook

A Mahayana Buddhist Approach to Death and Rebirth

Master YongHua

LU MOUNTAIN TEMPLE

Lu Mountain Temple
7509 Mooney Drive
Rosemead, CA 91770, USA
Tel: (626) 280-8801
First edition, ISBN 978-1502836762

www.ChanPureland.org
www.BLI2P.org

Contents

What If?

What if you could end all suffering and enjoy eternal bliss?

What if you could attain a permanent state of perfect happiness, without the duality of its opposite – pain?

What if you could break the cycle of reincarnation and continue your spiritual cultivation with a constant forward movement, never losing ground?

What if you could cultivate in a world of peace, where everyone around you supports your efforts, and you support theirs?

What if you could clear away the debris that prevents you from seeing your True Self, and that of all others?

What if you could realize your True Nature, become a Buddha, and realize the vow to help all living beings attain the same?

This is what the Buddhas promise us, if we cultivate our inner gardens and plant good strong seeds that take root and flourish.

The quest for enlightenment is a long and arduous spiritual journey that can take many lifetimes. But there is a shorter and more pleasurable path…

It is called the Pure Lands.

Introduction

About 2,500 years ago, there lived a man named Siddhartha Gautama who refused to accept suffering as an unalterable fact of his life. Instead, he vowed not to rest until he had attained perfect happiness.

After more than six years of vigorous cultivation met by bitter failure, finally his quest was successful; Siddhartha was able to end his suffering, and in the process he became enlightened: he woke up from the dream of his own ignorance and saw the True Nature of his mind.

After Siddhartha attained enlightenment, he reached a state of perfect wisdom and became known as Shakyamuni Buddha, or simply "The Buddha" – a Sanskrit title meaning "the Awakened One."

Fortunately for us, Shakyamuni discovered that he could also guide others to reach this perfect happiness, and he spent the remaining 50 years of his life teaching. Thus Shakyamuni became the historical founder of Buddhism.

The happiness that the Buddha discovered is so complete and perfect that, to be accurate, we really should not even use the word "happiness," since it cannot encompass the depth and wonder of this state. If we realized how blissful enlightenment is, we would all be striving for it. One cannot attain anything more valuable in this life.

Unfortunately, it is incredibly difficult to become enlightened, and most of us will not succeed in one lifetime. But we must not become discouraged. Instead, we should remember that attaining enlightenment has always been a multi-lifetime process, and it would be unreasonable to suppose otherwise.

Buddhism teaches that our current life is not the end of the road, but that after death we will be reincarnated into another body in accordance with the natural law of cause and effect. If we do good deeds, known as good karma, and plant good causes, or seeds, we will benefit. If we harm others and do evil, we will suffer in the future. But if we plant good seeds and practice diligently, then lifetime after lifetime, we can continue to progress until we, too, reach enlightenment.

However, we must also realize that reincarnation is an unpredictable and risky business: not only is it difficult to avoid creating offenses in this lifetime, but we also have to bear the consequences of offenses we created in past lives. Consequently, Buddhism teaches that after this life, many people will be reborn as ghosts, animals or even in the hells, where they will experience extreme suffering and hardship, and be set back on the path to enlightenment.

Thus we need a method that not only helps us improve in this lifetime, but also ensures that we will continue to progress in future lives. This is where the Pure Land Dharma Door comes in. "Dharma Door," here, refers to a method or style of practicing the teachings of the Buddha, which are known as the Dharma.

The Pure Land School is based on certain key sutras – recorded Buddhist teachings – that are especially effective in helping us navigate the dangers of reincarnation. For instance, in *The Buddha Speaks of Amitabha Sutra*, Shakyamuni teaches his disciples about another Buddha, named Amitabha, who resides in a distant world, or galaxy in modern terms, very far away from ours.

According to Mahayana Buddhism, one of the two main branches of Buddhism, Shakyamuni Buddha is only one of countless Buddhas who come to different worlds throughout the universe to teach living beings. Amitabha is another such Buddha, who made 48 great vows to help all beings attain rebirth to his world, the Western Bliss Pure Land, often referred to simply as the Pure Land.

Thanks to Amitabha's vows, we can draw on his power to help us reach his Pure Land. If we manage to be reborn there, we will find ourselves in a wonderful environment that is very blissful and supportive of cultivation. In Buddhism, "cultivation" refers to practicing Buddhist methods, or Dharmas, such as meditation, reciting of the Buddha's name, and many others.

Most importantly, if we make it to the Pure Land, we can be certain that we will attain enlightenment in *that very lifetime*, and that we will never have to suffer again.

Does this sound too good to be true?

There is a catch: it is not easy to successfully practice the Pure Land Dharma and be reborn to the Pure Land. Nonetheless, it is much easier to reach the Pure Land than to become enlightened in this lifetime.

Thus the Pure Land Dharma Door makes the Buddha's teachings more accessible to a wider range of people. That is why Pure Land is the most widely practiced form of Buddhism in the world today.

However, the Pure Land Dharma Door is still largely unfamiliar to most people in the West. As a result, the first goal of this book is to provide an accessible introduction to the Pure Land teachings, and also to Mahayana Buddhism in general.

The second goal of this book is to address some of the practical questions concerning the Pure Land Dharma that people have been asking us. Many of these questions were raised by members of our assembly during lectures, or by members of the online community who visit our website. I wish to thank all of these people for their participation, without which this book would not have been possible.

Finally, despite its great popularity, Pure Land Buddhism is misunderstood by the vast majority of those who practice it. For instance, many of those who are familiar with Pure Land Buddhism through their upbringing or culture, actually know very little about the proper teachings. Though they may follow the traditions with which they grew up, and they may look to a temple for support when their loved ones pass away, their understanding of Pure Land Buddhism is often reduced to a set of superstitions. Therefore, the third goal of this book is to correct some common misperceptions about the Pure Land Dharma.

Part I of this book will briefly outline the Buddhist solution to the problem of suffering by discussing cause and effect, reincarnation, enlightenment, and the path to Buddhahood. Parts II through V will explain the basic elements of the Pure Land approach, and Part VI will explain how to cultivate the Pure Land Dharma Door. Finally, Parts VII and VIII will add some closing thoughts, as well as a Question and Answer section that will address additional specific questions, and a glossary of important terms.

I am indebted to my teacher, the Great Master Xuan Hua, who brought Mahayana to the West from China in the 1960s; thus I have vowed to repay his kindness by becoming a teacher myself, hoping to pass on what I have learned to the next generation.

I have high hopes that many who study with us and learn to recite the Buddha's name will attain their desired objectives and accomplish their Way karmas.

Unlike most forms of Buddhism in this country, which have been simplified to suit Western sensibilities, the Great Master Hua's teachings draw on the full range of the Mahayana Dharma, and consequently some concepts may seem foreign to Westerners. However, our view is that many important parts of the Dharma were lost in this simplification. Therefore we encourage you to read on and keep an open mind, giving yourself a chance to discover the depth of the Buddha's original teachings, which have benefited countless people over the past 2,500 years.

I

Buddhism 101

1. Shakyamuni Buddha: Our Original Teacher

As we have already discussed, Shakyamuni Buddha is the founder of Buddhism. He is the most recent Buddha known to mankind. If you gaze at statues and images of "Buddha" that are found throughout the world, in temples, homes, and in gardens of disciples and of those who simply admire Asian art, more than likely you are looking at the likeness of Shakyamuni.

Shakyamuni, which means the "Sage of the Shakya clan," was born Siddhartha Gautama to a ruling family in what is now Nepal. At the time of his birth, more than 2,500 years ago, wise men predicted that Siddhartha would either become a great ruler, or a renunciant and a wise spiritual teacher.

Siddhartha's father, King Suddhodana, preferred that his son would follow in his footsteps and become a great ruler. Determined to guard against the prophecy that he would renounce his royal legacy the king decided to provide such an enjoyable life that Siddhartha would never want to leave.

Thus, from childhood to adulthood, Siddhartha was isolated from life outside the palace walls. Siddhartha married his first cousin, Princess Yasodhara, and together they lived in one of the several palaces that were built specially for them. However, shielding Siddhartha from the problems of the world did not bring him happiness. Instead, Siddhartha became disenchanted. With the king's reluctant approval, Siddhartha made four trips outside the palace walls, and these experiences changed his life.

During his first three explorations, Siddhartha encountered sickness, old age and death, which troubled him greatly. He asked himself, "How can I enjoy a life of pleasure when there is so much suffering in the world?" On his fourth trip, he encountered a monk who had given up his worldly possessions to find a way to end suffering. This monk so impressed Siddhartha that he decided to renounce his kingdom, his family, and all he owned, for the life of a wandering monk.

He now called himself merely, Gautama. He wore the ragged clothes of a beggar, and cut off his hair as a symbol of renunciation of worldly desires and pleasures. In his search for truth, Gautama met with the wisest teachers of his day, but no one could tell him how to end suffering. His outward search for wisdom ended, and he turned his focus inward. He practiced severe asceticism, adopting the then-prevailing belief that this would bring him wisdom. However, after six years of punishing self-deprivation, Gautama came to this realization: There is nothing to be won or gained by living in total luxury, or its complete opposite, severe asceticism. Gautama came to understand the philosophy of the "Middle Way." He stopped his extreme actions, began eating healthfully again, and regained his strength. Finding a balance, he was able to gain wisdom.

One day in the spring, Gautama sat beneath a Bodhi tree, and fell into deep meditation with an unwavering focus on ending suffering. For 49 long days, he fought back against attacks from Mara, the demon king. Mara was resolute on preventing Gautama from reaching enlightenment, and besieged him with storms, hail, and flaming rocks, but Gautama remained unmoving. Mara then sent armies of demons to attack Gautama. When this failed, Mara tried to tempt Gautama by sending his beautiful daughters to seduce him. But through his tempered virtue and merit, Gautama remained resolute. Because of his tremendous concentration power, he was able to successfully resist all of Mara's attacks.

After successfully passing the demons' tests, Gautama suddenly understood the cause of suffering in this world, and how to help others end suffering. Gautama had destroyed the shackles of his own ignorance, and attained complete and perfect enlightenment. He had become a Buddha, and had reached a state of such perfect wisdom, that he knew everything that can be known, both about living beings' minds, and about the functioning of the universe at large. From that moment on, Gautama went by the name of Shakyamuni Buddha, and he spent the next 50 years of his life propagating Buddhism.

When the Buddha became enlightened, he reached Nirvana, which is a Sanskrit word meaning "cessation" or "still extinction." Nirvana is a state of inconceivable freedom and bliss in which all suffering, as well as the normal functioning of the thinking mind, is ended. When the Buddha died, it is said that he "entered Nirvana," that is to say, freed from his body, he entered a state of complete peace so profound that it cannot be grasped by our rational mind.

But before he entered Nirvana, the Buddha designated The Venerable Maha Kashyapa as first patriarch of Orthodox Buddhism. Thus began a lineage of patriarchs responsible for the propagation and transmission of the Proper Dharma.

In AD 470, after a long decline of Buddhism in India, Patriarch Bodhidharma brought Orthodox Buddhism to China. Through the centuries, it spread across East Asia including Japan, Korea, Vietnam, Thailand, and Cambodia. In 1962, Patriarch Xuan Hua continued the work of the patriarchs and transmitted the Proper Dharma from China to the United States.

2. Suffering, That Unalienable Right

The Buddha's wisdom is unsurpassed in human history. Beginning with his profound understanding of the universe in general, and the natural world in particular – all living beings and all inanimate things – one of the first lessons that Shakyamuni Buddha imparted to humanity was the Truth of Suffering, which states that life as we usually know it is marked by suffering.

Is this pessimism on the Buddha's part? No. It is, in fact, a realistic view of the human condition without the rose-colored glasses many of us are trained to wear.

What ordinary people call "happiness" is at best temporal and impermanent. How long does your happiness last when you purchase or receive a gift? A day, a month, a year? Unrealized or fleeting expectation is one aspect of suffering. Personal pain, self-doubt, jealousy, grief and loss are among the many forms suffering takes in our lives.

Ultimately, however, Buddhism is not pessimistic at all; in fact, it is very optimistic, in that Buddhism teaches us how to overcome the problem of suffering and realize bliss, or true happiness. Ironically, most of our attempts to chase after happiness actually lead to unhappiness.

Our daily life is full of suffering, most of all from activities that we often associate with happiness or pleasure. Our sense organs crave earthly pleasures. The mind is constantly striving to satisfy our senses. It is said that all living beings live within their sensory organs, which are our bridge to the physical world. However, the happiness we seek consists both of pleasure and of its opposite, pain. Think of a two-sided coin. Just because we choose to look at the pleasurable side does not mean that displeasure does not exist.

Suffering may be classified into three types:

Suffering within Suffering: It is also called the suffering of the have-nots and those whose expectations continually fall short, resulting in constant disappointment. For example, someone who already has a hard time making ends meet could, on top of it, fall sick while having no health insurance. Therefore, the causes of suffering may multiply. Suffering compounds suffering. From lack can spring envy and jealousy, which can breed hatred.

Suffering of Decay: This refers to those who have wealth, but suffer devastating losses. For example, one may lose one's fortune and become destitute, homeless, jobless and lonely. Someone unfamiliar with hardship may be ill-equipped to deal with this type of suffering. We can suffer even more painful loss with the death of a loved one.

Suffering of the Life Process: We cannot avoid the cycle of birth and death, whether of our thoughts, or of our physical shell, the human body. We are born, grow old, get sick and inevitably die. No matter how much money we have, we cannot stop this inexorable march toward death. Isn't that suffering?

In addition to these three divisions, we can also classify suffering into eight types:

Birth: Birth is a painful process for both the mother and her child; Most women experience labor pains, and the child must experience the trauma of leaving the safe, secure environment of the womb.

The Chinese sages say that the experience of being born into this world is like ripping the shell off a live tortoise!

Aging: We all must face the loss of our youth and the inevitable bodily decay and mental deterioration. Physical suffering may arise from our body no longer being able to cope as we get older. We may have a hard time walking, our teeth may decay, our strength may decline, and we may suffer from other infirmities.

With age, we lose some mental acuity. We can become forgetful; we may not be able to sustain our train of thought and may experience mental deterioration. This is one mental aspect of suffering.

Sickness: Sickness will invariably befall all of us. And if we are physically tormented by illness, then our relatives and loved ones will likely suffer in the form of worry, sadness, or loss of sleep; they may even neglect their work because of our plight.

Death: Most of us are terrified of death. Even the sickest, most miserable among us have difficulty facing death, perhaps because we are attached to what we know, and fear the unknown.

Being Apart From the Ones We Love: We yearn to be with our loved ones, but at times we must be apart from them. Separation can be temporary as in travel, or permanent, as in death. In either case, the longing may cause great anxiety and suffering.

Being with Those We Hate: Often we must get together with those whom we loathe. There is a saying: "Seeing the enemy is like one's eyes being needled; being together with those we hate is like tasting bitter things and sleeping on a bed of nails."

Not Getting What We Want: We can wallow in misery when our desires and wishes are not fulfilled. The more acute the desire, the more bitter the disappointment when it is not fulfilled. Many of us do not achieve the fame, wealth or love to which we aspire.

The Suffering of the Raging Five Skandhas: Skandha is Sanskrit for "heap" or "pile." Our personas are defined by five aspects:

1. Form: physical shape
2. Feelings: of pleasure or pain
3. Thinking: our mental processing
4. Activity: the lower level thinking process, which is like a mental undercurrent of which we are normally not even aware
5. Consciousness: our awareness

These five skandhas tend to accumulate and overwhelm us, resulting in mental confusion.

The three and eight types of suffering we have mentioned here provide two different frameworks with which to look at our experience. But there are in fact countless types of suffering. If we can first awaken to the presence of suffering within ourselves, then we can eventually learn how to eliminate it completely.

This is the nature of the Buddhist teachings. We share our understanding with you. We suggest ways to improve your lives; if you are sincere and wish to make progress, you can learn how to do it.

The Buddha recognized the suffering in his own human existence, and resolved to put an end to it. Once he was enlightened, he accomplished his goal and thus was able to spend the next 50 years teaching others how to end suffering and attain bliss. Subsequently, many of the Buddha's disciples practiced what he taught, and they too attained Nirvana.

What is Nirvana? It is the state of perfect freedom and bliss that only the Buddhist sages can understand and realize. Although we may not fully understand what Nirvana is, it is sufficient to say that it is the highest goal, the most worthwhile accomplishment one can ever aspire to. We should not settle for anything less.

3. The Three Poisons

Before can we understand Buddhism's solution to the problem of suffering, we must first get a better understanding of the problem itself.

Three things can poison our minds: greed, anger and stupidity. When our actions are motivated by these poisons, or even if we sow these kinds of thoughts in our mind, we are bound to reap retributions that will cause suffering in the future. And yet, many people seem oblivious to the dangers of indulging in these three poisons.

The greedy mind is never satisfied. No matter how much we have, it never seems to be enough. The alcoholic wants just one more sip of the bottle. The rich tycoon wants another million dollars. Both are willing to go to extremes to get what they want. Human beings may be willing to commit much evil to satisfy their excessive greed.

If we cannot get what we want, anger typically arises. We direct our dissatisfaction at those who obstruct us. We blame them, and feel vindicated in punishing them for hindering us. Because of our anger, we may feel justified in harming others.

Stupidity arises from confusion or lack of clear thinking. We simply do not understand. As a result, we do stupid things that we later regret. In particular, many of us fail to consider the law of cause and effect, which states that all of our actions carry consequences, just as echo follows sound, or shadow follows form.

In order to counteract the Three Poisons of the mind, the Buddha taught precepts, samadhi and wisdom. Cultivating precepts will eradicate greed. Practicing Samadhi, or concentration, will counteract anger. Unfolding wisdom will dispel stupidity.

Precepts are the Buddhist rules of morality. The Five Precepts form the basis for all the other Buddhist precepts. They are:

1. No killing: We must not take others' lives, no matter how justified we feel.

2. No Stealing: To steal is to take another's property – material possessions, identity, spouse, another's ideas, etc. – without permission. Such behavior is destructive. Let's teach our own children not to steal, so that future generations may have a better chance to live in safety and harmony.

   Also at the time of this writing, Japan had just experienced a tsunami, and the ensuing nuclear disaster at Fukushima. Many people were displaced from their homes, and they lost most of their belongings. Amazingly, it was reported in the news that the Japanese people returned more than $70 million in cash found in the wreckage to their rightful owners. Japan's deep Buddhist tradition may have a lot to do with this most remarkable type of decency.

3. No Sexual Misconduct: Sexual misconduct refers to sexual activity outside of marriage. Breaking the marriage vow of fidelity invariably destroys bonds of trust, and in some cases, the marriage. Further, the Buddhists who observe the Five Precepts are taught not to engage in premarital sex.

4. No Lying: This ranges from small lies to big lies. As the Chinese say, a lie occurs when the mind says, "Yes" but the mouth says, "No" – in other words, when you know that your own statement is untrue.

   Habitual liars do not realize that they fool themselves first, in order to minimize their own internal conflict. Many are so absorbed in convincing themselves that their own lies are true, that they fail to recognize the signals that others do not believe their lies at all.

   How about the "successful" liars, those who get away with their lies? They tend to be very lonely because their lives lack integrity, and no one really trusts them. As Abraham Lincoln once said, "You can fool all the people some of the time, and some of the people all the time, but you cannot fool all the people all the time."

5. No Taking of Intoxicants. Intoxicants include alcohol, cigarettes, and drugs. Intoxicants cloud our minds and make us prone to breaking the previous four precepts. Thus the fifth precept is called a preventive precept.

   One of our disciples enjoys having a drink after work to relax. It makes her feel good. Many people would agree. There is no harm in one drink! Some

> studies even say that drinking one glass a day is good for your heart. However, alcohol is also a depressant, and in the long run, drinking is not beneficial to the cultivation of meditation and other spiritual practices. In particular, alcohol can cloud your mind and your judgment, whereas developing wisdom requires us to see clearly.
>
> If you want to relax, you can learn to meditate. (You can obtain a copy of *The Chan Handbook: The Learner's Guide to Meditation*, and learn the practice of meditation.) Studies have shown that meditation can reduce stress, improve your health, lower blood pressure and help you control your urge to overindulge in food and drink.

The first four precepts are called "precepts of the nature." To violate them would violate our True Nature. In other words, if we were not confused, we would not even have such thoughts, let alone act upon them. It should not be surprising that all the major religions of the world share the same characteristics as the first four precepts.

Observing precepts can give rise to samadhi. Samadhi is the Sanskrit word for proper concentration – the ability to focus on a single issue, and not be distracted by anything else. This is what enables the champion athlete to concentrate on the task at hand, instead of becoming distracted by the crowd's noises, or by the wind.

Buddhism has many advanced techniques to develop samadhi power. If you want to accomplish your ambitions in life, you must learn to focus your mind. Following the precepts, as well as meditation, are among the many tools that can help you develop the concentration necessary to achieve your ambitions.

When you have samadhi, you will not be affected by external distractions. You tend to be more balanced. Your mind will be steadier, and less prone to wide fluctuations. That is inner peace. That is the absence of anger. That is a state that most people cannot experience, unless they have some kind of spiritual pursuit.

Samadhi can unfold wisdom. Without adequate samadhi power, wisdom cannot possibly be opened. Buddhists believe that all of us have inherent wisdom. Cultivation is the process of unfolding the wisdom we already possess. And yes, even the most ignorant and deluded people can become wise because we all have the same inherent wisdom: that of the Buddha's.

Wisdom here refers to Prajna Wisdom, or transcendental wisdom, not simply "knowledge." The objective of Buddhism is to allow people to see and experience the Truth. How can you recognize people who have not yet experienced the Truth? They are often full of themselves. They often claim that they understand everything, are critical of others, and tend to be greedy for recognition and profit.

How can we recognize somebody who has wisdom?

Wise people can see their own faults. They therefore are more humble and do not resent others as much. They do not blame others. They do not look at others' faults. Then eventually, they develop a deeper understanding of cause and effect. That is how they can end all of their suffering and attain bliss.

In contrast, most of us are confused and deluded, and hence tend to blame others and ignore our own faults.

Finally, why do we want to eradicate the three poisons? Because, according to the sages:

- Greed plants the seeds for us to become hungry ghosts. These beings share the same world as ours, only we cannot see them, just as there are certain wavelengths of light that we cannot see. Hungry ghosts experience severe hunger and thirst as part of their existence.
- Anger makes us fall to the hells. According to Buddhism, the hells do exist; this is the last place you would want to be reborn in the future.
- Stupidity destines us to become animals.

Buddhism teaches that there are many other realms, aside from the familiar human realm. When our physical body dies, our soul, known as the Eighth Consciousness in Buddhism, will be reborn in a new body, and not necessarily in the human realm. Buddhism teaches that the Three Poisons create the causes for us to fall into the lower realms of animals, ghosts, or to the hells. These three realms are referred to as the three "evil paths" because they are the prime destinations for those who commit evil acts. The lower realms are dreadful places to be because they are very hard to leave, and everyone who is reborn there will experience unspeakable suffering for many, many lifetimes.

Some readers may be skeptical of these teachings. For those who wish to continue reading, we suggest you do so with an open mind. In time you may come to resonate with these teachings and see their benefits. If not, you can always choose to set aside Buddhism's metaphysical claims and focus only on practical techniques, such as meditation which can provide many positive health benefits as well as a sense of peace and well-being.

4. Cause and Effect

To resolve the problem of suffering, we must first understand the principle of cause and effect.

Throughout the universe, nothing changes haphazardly. Everything follows a common rule. That rule is cause and effect, often mistakenly referred to as karma. However, technically, the term karma only means action, be it physical or mental; at its root karma refers to the mental intentions or volitions that form the basis of our actions.

Buddhism teaches that every action will cause a particular effect, known as a karmic retribution, to arise in the future. Conversely, everything we are currently experiencing is caused by prior actions, or karma that we created in the past. This correlation between cause and effect is a universal law, and not random.

The law of cause and effect requires neither giver, nor creator, but rules quietly and impartially. If we wish to resolve the problem of suffering and attain enlightenment, then we must understand cause and effect.

One of my students said that he wished that Buddhism could be more scientific, because he needed more facts to deepen his faith. I suggested he look at Newton's Third Law of Motion, which states: "To every action there is always an equal and opposite reaction." This is an elegant statement of cause and effect. What could be more scientific than that?

In the context of karma, we can state the concept of equal and opposite reactions like this: Do good and you will receive blessings. Do evil and you will definitely suffer evil consequences. In other words, "What goes around, comes around."

Blessings are like the currency in our karmic bank account. When we have enough money in our bank account, we can buy the things we want. Likewise, if we have a lot of blessings in our karmic account, then good things will naturally come to us. On the other hand, if we have harmed many people in the past, then our account will be in the red, and eventually bad things will happen to us, until we manage to pay off our debts. In fact, we all have a combination of good and bad karma.

The forces of cause and effect not only shape the events of our present lifetime, but they also dictate how we will fare after death, and how we came to be born where we are now.

The next chapter will look more closely at reincarnation. For now, just know that we became human beings because, in past lifetimes, we planted the seeds to do so. Those seeds are known in Buddhism as the Five Precepts, which we explained in Chapter 3.

Similarly, we can plant seeds to become gods or heavenly beings in future lifetimes by practicing the Ten Good Deeds, the first four of which are committed with the mouth, the next three with the mind, and the final three with the body:

1. No harsh speech
2. No lying

3. No double-tongued speech
4. No frivolous speech (such as gossip)
5. No greed
6. No hatred
7. No stupidity
8. No killing
9. No stealing
10. No sexual misconduct

When we understand the connections between cause and effect, we will know the best ways to act. For instance, those who are not greedy or stingy will not be weighed down by money and material circumstances; they will be more content, and at peace. Those who are not angry tend to have a more harmonious family life. Those who do not indulge in desires usually have clear minds and healthy bodies.

However, many people fail to see clearly and do not understand the connection between cause and effect. Consequently, they are easily confused by appearances, are often self-absorbed, and like to indulge themselves. In the process, they behave inappropriately, and create offenses against the people around them. That is why most of them are unhappy and afflicted.

In Buddhism, we refer to people who love to fight as asuras[1]. Those with the asura nature tend to be very

---

[1] The asuras are one of the six realms of rebirth, alongside the hell, ghost, animal, human, and heavenly realms.

afflicted, and are often looking to pick fights. In contrast, the Buddha was not angry or confrontational, because he was confident in his own understanding. When you are truly right, there is no need to defend or justify yourself to others.

Having accomplished perfect enlightenment, there is nothing that the Buddha does not know. He is able to clearly understand the law of cause and effect that governs the universe. Cause refers to the root action or event that leads to a certain result, or effect. The cause embodies the force or energy that drives the process. The effect represents the materialization of this driving force. Both cause and effect are inextricably interrelated. There is no effect without a cause, and conversely, there is no cause without an effect.

We should keep in mind a few characteristics regarding this law: "Such is the cause, such is the effect." In other words, the general type of effect is predetermined by each cause, just as the fruit corresponds to the type of seeds that one plants. The cause is the seed, and the effect is the fruit. So if you inflict pain on others, you will have to undergo pain yourself in the future.

Conversely, the cause embodies an essence of the fruit, as surely as DNA shapes each living creature. In fact, cause and effect can be linked in a continuous chain, in which each effect becomes the cause for the next effect, as in chemical reactions.

The specific manifestations of a particular effect, however, are not predetermined because they also depend on "aiding conditions" that influence exactly how and when the effect will occur. For example, during the growth process of a plant, there are aiding conditions that influence the development of the fruit; once the seed has been planted, the proper amount of sun, water, and nutrients, as well as the right temperature, are needed for the tree to grow and bear fruit. Thus, the progression from cause to effect can be slow or fast depending on the situation.

If we understand and believe in the law of cause and effect, then we can eliminate superstition and confusion; we will understand that everything happens for a reason, and that our future is determined by our own actions rather than the whims of others, or by a supreme being.

If we have faith in the law of karma, then we can recognize that the suffering we face in our lives is not random. Rather, it is the consequence of evil actions that we have done in the past, whether in this life or a prior one. This understanding enables us to see that the suffering we are going through is not senseless. There is a reason behind it, and thus we can learn from it. This approach can help us accept the suffering we must go through in this life.

Nothing makes our suffering worse than if we try to reject it and live in a constant state of denial. Acceptance can be very helpful. If we understand cause and effect, when situations do not turn out as we wish, we can know that the causes lie in the past. Then we can stop blaming others for our troubles and difficulties, and we need not despair.

The acceptance of suffering, however, is not the end goal of our practice, since the aim of Buddhist cultivation is to become free of all suffering. But realistically, we must experience a certain amount of suffering before we can accomplish this goal.

As my teacher Great Master Xuan Hua often said:

To endure suffering is to end suffering.
To enjoy blessings is to exhaust our blessings.

The suffering that we experience is simply the retribution that we must undergo to repay our karmic debts. The good news is that the more suffering we endure, the more we pay off our karmic debts, and the quicker our troubles and difficulties will end.

One can look at it this way: each of us has a certain amount of bad karma that we will have to go through eventually, so we might as well get it out of the way now. This understanding can make the suffering much easier to bear.

In addition, for those who truly have faith, Buddhism offers many tools that go beyond acceptance and can actually resolve our karmic debts. For instance, we can dedicate merit and blessings toward helping those whom we may have harmed in the past; we can bow to the Buddhas in repentance; or we may simply do good for others and thereby plant seeds for good things to happen to us in the future. These kinds of practices can alleviate our suffering.

Furthermore, understanding the law of cause and effect can help us have faith in humanity, knowing that good things will happen to those who do good, and who plant the proper seeds for advancement.

There is an ancient Chinese saying: “One man creates merit, a thousand benefit from it.” For example, a tree blooms and the surrounding trees can also enjoy its fragrance. A bee’s simple act of pollination ensures growth and fertilization which benefits nature beyond a single flower. Similarly, when we do good, those around us will benefit as well.

If we understand the law of cause and effect, we will be more careful in our actions, knowing we should refrain from evil and practice only good.

Finally, we must harness the law of cause and effect on our path to enlightenment. In particular, in our practice, we must plant the right kinds of causes that will eventually germinate and produce awakening. For instance, by helping others along the path to enlightenment, we plant the causes for others to help us reach awakening in the future.

In addition, the Pure Land method of reciting Amitabha's name, which we will discuss in Part VI, is another good example of this application of cause and effect. The more we recite Amitabha's name, and the more Samadhi, or concentration, we apply to our recitation, the more we plant causes for our eventual rebirth to the Pure Land.

5. Reincarnation

Some people believe that upon death, we disappear altogether: we simply return to the dust. This is a form of nihilism.

In contrast, others believe that our soul's existence is permanent: for example, they may believe that after death they can go up to the heavens and enjoy heavenly blessings forever, which is a common form of eternalism. Generally, eternalism is the belief that the self or soul has a fixed and essential nature that is eternal and cannot be destroyed.

In Buddhism, we take the Middle Way, and believe that our soul neither disappears entirely, nor exists permanently unchanged – rather, each soul cycles through reincarnation. We go through countless births and deaths as a result of our karma.

Reincarnation comes from the Sanskrit term samsara. Samsara is often translated as the "reincarnation wheel." A wheel usually embodies circular as well as vertical motion. The image of a wheel symbolizes how all living beings are born into various locations in the universe, and go through the various planes of existence non-stop – some high, some low, just like a wheel. It also symbolizes the fundamental, unbroken chain of cause and effect that dictates what types of bodies we will obtain each time we go through birth and death.

Everything in the universe goes through cycles of change. The evolution of living beings through the cycle of reincarnation is a dynamic process much like the changes that occur in the natural world around us.

Consider the four great elements of earth, water, wind, and fire which pass through natural changes in their states of being.

Take the element of earth. Originally, it is simply dirt. Then the potter molds it and bakes it into a vessel. Over time, the vessel gets destroyed and thus eventually returns to its original state of dirt.

Water has its own cycles, beginning with evaporation from the oceans and lakes. Vapor then ascends to the skies, where it is cooled and condenses into clouds. Clouds gather and eventually the water falls to earth as rain, returning to the original state of a liquid. And then the cycle begins again.

The wind element is just movement of air. Air is heated by the sun, expands and ascends to the skies, creating empty space. The low pressure of empty space causes air from other areas to be moved toward it, thus causing wind. The air movement can be slow or fast, creating gentle wind or violent tornadoes.

The great fire element originates from heat. When conditions allow, heat can create fire. Potential heat already exists in all things and waits for conditions to manifest itself in the form of fire. For example, two wood sticks already contain heat in the form of energy stored in their molecular structure. When we rub them together, heat will manifest and create fire. In other words, fire also cycles through various states of manifestation, which may be visible or invisible to our eyes.

Our bodies are the result of the temporary union of these four great elements. For example, the great earth element gives our body solidity in the form of bones, muscles etc. The great water element constitutes our blood, tears etc. Our breathing and rhythms of the heart are based on the great wind element. Finally, our body heat is derived from the great fire element. Like the four constituent elements, our body must also go through reincarnation as driven by the forces of karma.

On a larger scale, each galaxy, which in Buddhism is known as a world, must also cycle through a kind of reincarnation. Each world must go through the four cycles of formation, dwelling, decay and emptiness. More specifically, each world first comes into existence, then reaches maturity, deteriorates, and finally disappears. Throughout the universe, one world comes into existence while others disappear in a wonderful cadence that is dictated by the laws of cause and effect.

Ordinary living beings cycle through the following six planes of existence as driven by the karma they have created:

The hell realms: Yes, the hells do exist. These are the last places that you want to be in.

The hells are characterized by extreme suffering. The prisoners there undergo constant torture through very lengthy terms. At the end of such terms, they tend to be reborn into the hells to continue undergoing their retribution.

How do we fall to the hells? If in this life, we plant the causes for going to the hells, then after our death, we will most likely be reborn there. In particular, succumbing to anger creates the seeds for falling into the hells. We'll elaborate further in a later section.

The hungry ghosts' realm: Buddhism teaches that there are ghosts and spirits just as there are humans. Ghosts are predominantly yin beings; yin is the dark force that opposes yang in traditional Chinese philosophy and medicine. These beings are in great suffering because they are constantly thirsty and hungry. You have no idea what it is like until you have no water to drink or food to eat. It feels so bad that you want to die but you can't! Ghosts exist in the midst of our human world. However, we cannot usually see them because they are outside the range of our everyday perceptions, just like infrared light or radio waves, which exist at wavelengths that we cannot perceive.

How do we become hungry ghosts? If we harbor a greedy mind, we will plant the causes for receiving a hungry ghost body in the future.

The animal realm: The animal, ghost, and hell realms are together commonly referred to as the "three evil paths," because there is a lot of suffering there, the terms are very long and it is very hard to escape these realms.

How do we obtain an animal body? By planting the causes of stupidity. Just indulge in excessive sensual pleasures, live senselessly, surrender to your ego and you will definitely fall to this realm.

The asura realm: Asuras are present both in their own realm, which is a separate plane of existence from ours, and in all the other realms as well. Asuras are fond of fighting, arguing, and conflict for its own sake. For example, many asuras in our human realm become soldiers, boxers, or anyone with a combative nature. Even many established and respected professionals are asuras. You can recognize their asura nature immediately because they often contradict those around them, and insist on offering their opinion, even if unsolicited.

The Buddha predicted that after his death, the world would gradually decline. We see a pattern of conflict in our world today, and disharmony among cultures, religions, political groups and even youth. Few people devote their lives to practicing virtue, and many prefer, instead, to fight. Asuras are common in today's world.

The human realm: Humans are a mixture of yin and yang, a combination of goodness and evil. The human realm, as well as the subsequent heavenly realms, are much more conducive to cultivation than the other four types of rebirth.

In order to obtain a human body, we should cultivate the Five Precepts.

The heavenly realms: You plant the causes for birth to the heavens by cultivating the Ten Good Deeds and observing the Five Precepts.

In the heavens, everything is as you wish. You are reborn in the heavens because you have earned enough blessings that now you can sit back and enjoy them. The heavens are very blissful. The only drawback is that it is not a permanent solution. In time, those in the heavens will use up all of their blessings and fall back down to lower realms again, and the cycles of rebirth will continue.

These are the six common realms. In order to get out of the cycle of reincarnation, one must cultivate diligently to make it to the four sagely realms of the Arhats, Pratyekabuddhas, Bodhisattvas and Buddhas. These different levels of wisdom will be discussed in Chapters 8 and 9.

But first, let us look at some of the evidence in support of reincarnation.

There was a noted doctor who became a believer in reincarnation after one of his patients recalled past life traumas that assisted in relieving the anxieties and phobias she was experiencing in her life. His belief strengthened after seeing many more patients regress to past lives.

This doctor, who graduated from Columbia University and Yale Medical School, was using both traditional therapy and hypnosis to help his patient overcome her symptoms. During hypnotic states, she experienced a series of past lives, and was able to speak to higher beings in an "in-between lives" state.

In addition, during a hypnotic state, the patient connected with the doctor's dead father and son, and related to to doctor that his son had died in infancy due to a rare heart condition. This was information she could not have known and the doctor became convinced his patient had tapped into another realm.

Here are some other stories of reincarnation.

In the first half of the 20th century in Delhi, India, lived an 8-year old girl named Phatedevin. She often cried and begged her parents to allow her to go to Mita, another city that was 120 miles away, so that she could see her husband.

Perplexed, her parents asked a journalist to investigate the matter.

Phatedevin told the reporter that, in her past life, she had been married to a teacher and bore him a son. When their son was 11 years old, she fell sick and passed away. When the reporter pressed her for proof, she said that she buried gold, silver and jewels at specific locations. She also told him about a gift of a fan that bore some specific writings and was given to her by a friend.

The reporter went to Mita and found the teacher and confirmed that the teacher's wife had passed away nine years previously. He also verified everything the girl had claimed including the existence of the fan with the writings.

The reporter returned to Delhi and brought the girl and her parents back to Mita. Even though she had never left Delhi before, she was able to navigate the city streets of Mita and led them to the teacher's house.

As they entered the house, they met with an 80-year old man with white hair. The young girl was very happy and indicated that he had been her father-in-law. She also was able to recognize her previous husband and son.

This was reported in the major newspapers in India and many more newspapers in the world.

There is another remarkable story about an Englishwoman named Jenny Cockell, who as a child, recalled a previous life in Ireland as a woman named Mary Sutton. Sutton died in childbirth, leaving behind eight children.

As a young girl, Jenny spoke of her life in Ireland, and even drew a map of the small village where she was born; she could also describe the room where she had died in 1936. As a child, she was obsessed with making sure that the children from her previous life were all right.

After her death as Mary Sutton, her children had been sent to orphanages. As an adult, in her current life, Cockell was able to obtain six of her children's names with the help of a priest from an orphanage in Ireland.

In 1993, Cockell was able to track down her five surviving children and reunite with them during the filming of an Irish documentary about her journey. Cockell wrote a book about her story called "Across Time and Death." The story was dramatized in a CBS movie made for television in 2000.

The final incident we will refer to is a rather atypical occurrence of rebirth where one person's consciousness was reborn, not into the body of a newborn baby, but into another adult. It occurred in Cà Mâu, Vietnam, in the prior century, where a girl fell ill and died at the age of 19 in the small village of Đầm Giơi. At another village of Vĩnh Mỹ (Bạc Liêu), there was at the same time a girl who was sick, but recovered. After she recovered, she no longer recognized her parents and behaved strangely. Her parents initially thought that this was probably due to side effects from her illness. When fully recovered, she started crying and insisted on getting permission to return to the village of Đầm Giơi which she could describe in minute detail.

Her parents contacted the people of the Đầm Giơi village and came across the family of the young girl who had died in Đầm Giơi; they invited the family to come for a visit. As soon as they arrived in Vĩnh Mỹ, the daughter recognized the visitors as her own parents and shared family secrets that no one else could know. Eventually, she was recognized by both families and inherited their fortunes.

This was widely circulated in Vietnamese newspapers.

Some may be skeptical about the reality of reincarnation. But try to keep an open mind to the possibility that our consciousness has been migrating from body to body for a long time, propelled by causal forces that we created in the past.

If we have faith that reincarnation is real, then we would be wise to refrain from creating offenses in order to avoid falling to the lower realms, because once we have fallen, there is a lot of suffering and it is extremely difficult to extricate ourselves.

Further, we should make the effort to do good deeds in order to plant the causes for ascension so that we can one day escape the cycle of suffering and attain bliss – a central aim for the Buddhist cultivator.

6. Lessen Desires, Know Contentment

How do you recognize a true Buddhist? He or she has few desires and is easily satisfied.

In Buddhism, seeking benefits and advantages for this life is regarded as a "worldly" aim. Those who are worldly tend to be competitive, chase after material things, and never seem to be satisfied. While it may be understandable for the "have-nots" to be greedy, paradoxically the "haves" seem to be even greedier.

The Chinese have an expression: "Greedy as if one never has enough." The Vietnamese would say: "Greed is bottomless." They would also say: "The great ocean may be filled, but not the greedy mind."

This is why the Buddha taught his disciples to "moderate [their] desires, and know contentment." This is the basis for happiness, peace and bliss.

The spirit of Buddhist practice is moderation. To lessen desires is to avoid excessive indulgence. Those who cultivate tend to be more moderate.

To know contentment is to make do and be more accepting of our circumstances, even if they are lacking. For example, if we can be content with the material things we have, we will consequently become free of the torment resulting from unmet wants and desires.

Unless we are enlightened, all of us are attached to the following "Five Desires," which are rooted in our five senses:

1. Form: Desire arises when our eyes encounter forms that can be seen, ranging from alluring material objects to people. Buddhism teaches that the desire for beautiful forms is grounded in our biological desire for the opposite sex.

2. Sound: We enjoy pleasurable sounds. Some of us have a hard time getting a favorite tune out of our mind, which can take over our thoughts. Some people are addicted to words of praise.

3. Smell: Scent can trigger strong associations of nostalgia and desire, as evidenced by the proliferation of fragrances on the market.

4. Taste: Most of us include great food in the definition of the good life. In this day and age, people often overindulge in eating. This is one of the most difficult forms of addiction to overcome. As the Buddha said: "Living beings cannot leave the ground, nor live apart from trees and grass, because our food is produced by the earth, and therefore our bodies are heavy."

5. Touch: Human beings crave the touch of other people, which can also become a sensuous distraction. We also enjoy touching objects of various textures because it is simply pleasant.

The five senses can generate desires of excess that distract us from our path. As long as such desires have a hold on us, our lives revolve around scheming to satisfy them. There is danger in allowing ourselves to indulge. If we are reduced to being the slaves of our desire, we will stop at nothing to fulfill it. As Gordon Gecko uttered in the movie *Wall Street*: "Greed, for lack of a better word, is good!"

We should realize that the five desires are not our friends. They can cause more harm than good, and can lead to worry, fear, sadness, or anger. Efforts to satisfy our desire, either as individuals, or a society, can lead to fighting, cheating and war.

How can we feel good about ourselves if our "happiness" is derived from the suffering of others?

Moreover, once one desire is satisfied, how often can we manage to stop desiring more? More often than not, our desires continue to grow. When will we awaken to the fact that the greedier we are, the more we suffer?

This is why the true Buddhist takes heed of the Buddha's advice. He instructed his followers to moderate their desire so that they may be at peace and experience bliss under any circumstances.

Even though they may be materially rich, those who do not know contentment may feel very poor. In contrast, those who know contentment still feel satisfied and blissful, even if they must sleep on the floor, or endure hardships.

Wealth is a state of mind. If we can keep our greedy mind in check, that is being rich. If we cannot control our desires and urges, then we are very poor indeed.

To lessen desire and know contentment is the beginning of freedom, and puts us on the road to liberation. If everyone followed this principle, it would bring peace and bliss to the world, since we would no longer need to engage in struggle and conflict.

A good life must be balanced. Today, there is an imbalance between material life and spiritual life. When morality is sacrificed for the sake of material advancement, humanity comes closer to the brink of destruction. People who are overly preoccupied with the pursuit of material things do not know true happiness

To lessen desires and know contentment is to practice moderation in our daily life. That is the Buddhist way. But even once we reach contentment, this is just the beginning; there is so much more that we can accomplish on the path to enlightenment.

7. Enlightenment: The Dharma Door of Emptiness

As we have seen, a Dharma Door is a method. Practices such as meditation, reciting the Buddha's name, following precepts, etc. are all examples of Dharma Doors. One can also see a Dharma Door as a threshold that we must pass through in order to get to our destination.

Buddhism is a collection of Dharma Doors to Emptiness. It contains a set of methodologies to help living beings realize the Truth. When we see the truth of Emptiness, then we will attain liberation.

What is liberation? Clearly, we would like to be released from suffering and torments. However, true liberation requires freeing ourselves from happiness as well. As this idea may seem counter-intuitive, let us explore it further.

We live in a world of duality. Everything is defined in pairs of opposites. For example, rich is defined as not poor, strength is the absence of weakness, goodness is devoid of evil and so forth. Rarely can we find anything that is absolute. Everything is defined relative to its opposite. Confused people often choose to focus on one side, instead of taking a broader view.

Take love, for example. Love is the opposite of hate and is only a temporary state. In fact, within love there already is the seed for hate. We may be deeply in love with one another. But at the same time, we may already harbor the potential for great hatred should we be betrayed. The hatred is already present in great love. It does not appear from out of nowhere. It remains hidden under great love, until conditions warrant its appearance.

Similarly, happiness, also contains the seeds of unhappiness. Therefore, wise people are attached to neither suffering nor happiness. That is liberation. To clarify, Buddhism does not advocate becoming robots without love, feelings, or emotions. We advocate learning to live with minimal attachments. If good things happen, we appreciate them, but we do not demand more. If bad things occur, we do not mind and do not insist on rejecting them. That is freedom from duality.

This is not an intellectual exercise. Rather, it is a spontaneous state of mind that must be learned, until it becomes second nature. There is no mental processing involved. For example, when one's mind is even and one no longer gets excited about things, it is similar to how someone who used to be addicted to nicotine no longer gets agitated around cigarettes once they have managed to kick the habit.

Unlike us, Buddhas are free from duality. That is why they know the Truth. This is commonly referred to as the Buddha Nature. The Buddhas wish for all of us to share in their knowledge and views. However, this is only possible if we can see our own Buddha Nature and thus become enlightened.

The Buddha Nature is inherent in everyone and we will all eventually become Buddhas. But for now, we are still confused about the Truth and must go through the process of unraveling it. Once we rise above our confusion, we will see that inherently, we are all endowed with the enlightened nature. We just do not know how to access or use it while we are still deluded.

Enlightenment is the realization that fundamentally we are Empty.

This is not something that can be grasped through thought or reasoning; it is a realization that we must experience with our body and mind. This state is called True Emptiness: there is absolutely nothing there. It is also called Wonderful Existence: everything is contained within it.

Does it sound confusing? That is because it is something that cannot be described in words; rather, this is something you must realize for yourself.

Maybe that is why those who are enlightened never say that they are enlightened. If they claim that they are enlightened, then they have not really realized True Emptiness. If there is absolutely nothing there, how could they possibly claim there is something called enlightenment? If they still think there is something called enlightenment that can be described, then they have not actually realized True Emptiness, have they?

What does this mean to the rest of us, totally unenlightened mortals?

We too can realize True Emptiness. But in order to experience that state, we must cultivate.

While this is not easy, many cultivators have succeeded. In fact, there are countless Bodhisattvas who are enlightened.

We only have to find them and learn from them. They are eager to teach those who are qualified and sincere.

How can we recognize them? They are often referred to as Good Knowing Advisers. They are wise teachers who know how to guide us toward liberation.

But they will not knock on your door and plead to help you, First, you must do something that proves that you are worthy of being helped. Remember, confused people think highly of themselves.

How can you recognize a Good Knowing Adviser? Our *Chan Handbook* elaborates further on this topic, but the short answer is: you do not have to worry about it. If you simply work on making yourself worthy of being taught, wise teachers will recognize your potential and will teach you accordingly.

Wise teachers take your interest to heart. They are not doing it for themselves. Rather, they truly want to teach you, so that you can become a Buddha yourself one day. Good teachers demand action. They want results. They help by teaching you how to overcome impediments and obstacles to your progress. In other words, everything they ask of you is only for your benefit, not to make themselves rich or famous.

Those who are on the right path are happier, more blissful and find more meaning in life. They grow in humility, kindness, compassion, and generosity, and become less self-absorbed. They truly care for others. They are on the way to realizing True Emptiness.

Once True Emptiness is realized, what then? When we can see that everything is empty, we will no longer be attached.

By dropping our attachments, wc can lighten our load. Then we will really be able to let go and find true freedom.

Those who become enlightened are no longer attached to money, fame, food, or even their own body. They see that all conditioned phenomena are like a dream – impermanent and empty; they do not really exist. For instance, when someone is enlightened, they will be able to see the leg pain that occurs when meditating in the lotus position as empty; as soon as they recognize that the pain is not real, and not even their legs are real, then they will be able to stop the pain, if they choose.

Those who see emptiness are no longer afflicted by gain or loss, health or sickness, life or death. They have attained an unshakable happiness that does not depend on external conditions. And they will no longer be shackled by the cycle of reincarnation, but actually can have some control over their own birth and death. Thus they are truly free and at ease.

The technical Buddhist term for enlightenment is Nirvana. Those who attain Nirvana will see that True Emptiness is Wonderful Existence, and will experience a state of incredible bliss and total freedom that far surpasses any happiness that we can attain through our sensory organs.

We all have the same Buddha Nature, and hence we all have the capacity to reach Nirvana. However, attaining enlightenment is a tremendous achievement and is very difficult to do. Furthermore, there are many levels of enlightenment. So even once one reaches Nirvana, this is only the beginning. There is still so much refinement that is needed before one can reach the perfect wisdom of a Buddha.

8. Hinayana and Mahayana Buddhism

Hinayana and Mahayana are the two major branches of Buddhism. Mahayana is a Sanskrit term that means "great vehicle." The teachings of Mahayana are similar to a large ship that can ferry many living beings across the ocean of suffering to the other shore of Nirvana. These teachings elaborate on the tools that enable Bodhisattvas to save living beings on a broad scale. Hinayana means "small vehicle" because this approach is narrower and focuses primarily on pursuing enlightenment for oneself[2].

Theravadan Buddhism, which is prominent in Southeast Asian countries such as Sri Lanka, Thailand, and Cambodia, is typically regarded as Hinayana, and the terms "Hinayana" and "Theravadan" are often used interchangeably.

The Theravadan school is based on the early teachings of the Buddha, known as sutras, which were recorded in the vernacular Pali language. Mahayana Buddhism is based on

---

[2] Some people avoid the term "Hinayana" and regard it as derogatory. However, it is used here not in a derogatory sense, but because it conveys the greater breadth and different focus of the Mahayana teachings. In addition, we use the term "Hinayana" to remain consistent with the language used in the Buddhist Sutras and commentaries.

the more extensive collection of sutras recorded in the Sanskrit language, which is a more scholarly form of Pali. Whereas the Hinayana teachings only contain a subset of the full range of teachings and sutras that are included in the Mahayana canon, the Mahayana teachings include the entire Hinayana canon. This is another reason why Hinayana Buddhism is known as the "small vehicle."

However, it is worth noting that the essence of the term "Hinayana" actually is not tied to the Theravadan, or any other particular school or sect of Buddhism. Rather, Hinayana can be taken to refer to any practice of Buddhism that focuses primarily on one's individual practice, rather than on benefiting all living beings on a vast scale.

Given this understanding, many forms of Pure Land Buddhism, as well as the Zen practice that exists in the West, are actually Hinayana in nature, despite their official designation as Mahayana, because they primarily teach ways to benefit oneself, and do not teach how to save all living beings.

The central aims of Buddhist cultivation are: 1) to end suffering and obtain bliss; and 2) to become enlightened and liberate countless sentient beings.

Hinayana Buddhism focuses on the first of these goals: ending one's own suffering and attaining bliss. In order to accomplish this, we must empty our ego, since the ego is the root source of all suffering. Thus the Hinayana teachings focus on methods to extinguish the ego.

Mahayana practitioners also strive to empty the ego. However, Mahayana is distinguished by its emphasis on the second goal of Buddhism: becoming enlightened and learning how to liberate countless sentient beings.

According to the Mahayana teachings brought to us by Great Master Xuan Hua, as well as other Mahayana Patriarchs, emptying the self is not yet enlightenment; rather, it is an essential prerequisite that one must accomplish before one can become enlightened.

Thus Mahayana cultivators do not stop once they have emptied their ego, but rather aspire to go further and see their True Self (also known as the Buddha Nature). Those who succeed will attain the wisdom of a Bodhisattva and reach the various stages of enlightenment.

We will examine the path of the Bodhisattva in the following chapter; the remainder of this chapter will explore essential Hinayana teachings.

Both Hinayana and Mahayana practitioners begin their cultivation with the study of morality and the precepts. Moral conduct is the basis of concentration, or samadhi.

Subsequently, both Hinayana and Mahayana cultivators strive to increase their samadhi power through meditation and other practices.

The proper practice of morality and concentration will enable cultivators to empty the self and end their own suffering. Those who can do this are said to have accomplished the level of an Arhat, which is the primary goal of Hinayana Buddhism.

In Sanskrit, the word 'Arhat' means "sound hearer." These sages typically end their own suffering by listening to the Buddha (i.e. hearing his sound) and following his guidance.

When the term Arhat is used by itself, it actually refers to a Fourth Stage Arhat. Both Hinayana and Mahayana recognize three prior stages, known as the First through Third Stages of Arhatship, through which one must pass before becoming a Fourth Stage Arhat. These stages are explained in our various sutras, such as *The Earth Store Sutra.*

The Dharma to attain Arhatship is primarily based on the Four Noble Truths of:

1. Suffering
2. Accumulation
3. Extinction
4. The Way

According to the First Noble Truth, the Truth of Suffering, unless we can attain real wisdom, our existence is usually full of suffering.

According to the Second Truth, the Truth of Accumulation, suffering is caused by the accumulation of our desires and attachments: our desires have a way of accruing. When they are not satisfied, as is often the case, we suffer. Consequently, our suffering also accumulates, and we find ourselves buried beneath a tangled web of difficulties and problems from which it is very hard to free ourselves.

According to Third Noble Truth, the Truth of Extinction, there is a state called Nirvana, in which there is no suffering. Nirvana is also known as enlightenment, and is characterized by the four qualities of permanence, purity, True Self and bliss.

Finally, according to the Fourth Noble Truth, The Truth of the Way, there is a path to Nirvana, which the Buddhists know as the Middle Way. Follow it and you can cross over the sea of birth and death and reach the "other shore" of

Nirvana, leaving "this shore," the shore of suffering, far behind.

Besides Arhats, Pratyekabuddhas are another type of sage in Hinayana. They are also called the Conditioned Enlightened or the Solitarily Enlightened. One can reach the state of a Pratyekabuddha by investigating the following Twelve Conditioned Links, which explain how the cycle of birth and death originates, and also correspond to the stages of embryonic development:

1. Ignorance: The first link, ignorance, manifests itself as sexual desire or related forms of desire.
2. Activity: Desires lead to sexual activity.
3. Consciousness: Due to sexual activity, conception occurs. Human consciousness is described as having 8 components, known as The 8 Levels of Consciousness. At the time of conception, the eighth consciousness, also referred to as the soul, is the first of these components to arrive.
4. Name and Form: Once consciousness arrives, the fetus begins to form.
5. Six Entrances: Next the human body takes shape, and the sensory organs begin to function.
6. Contact: The sense organs make contact with the external world.
7. Feeling: When our senses contact the world, feelings of pleasure or pain arise.
8. Love: We love intense pleasant feelings and seek after them. Sometimes this link is translated as "craving" or "desire," however love more accurately captures the Buddha's insight into the nature of suffering.
9. Grasping: This love causes us to grasp at pleasant sensations and form heavy attachments.

10. Existence: Heavy attachments are the major forces that inexorably impel us to become what we wish. We thus wander from one plane of existence to another.
11. Birth: We are born into a new plane of existence.
12. Old Age and Death: Once we are born, we will inevitably grow old and die.

To understand the Twelve Links and end the cycle of reincarnation, Pratyekabuddhas retreat to the wilderness. They practice by themselves, contemplate the changing seasons, and observe the fleeting nature of life. Once they understand the Twelve Conditioned Links, they achieve awakening by undoing these successive links of causation in reverse order, until they come all the way back to the first one: ignorance. By ending ignorance, they can destroy the root source of all suffering and death, and thus attain liberation.

Those who accomplished the level of a Pratyekabuddha while the Buddha was still in the world, are known as Conditioned Enlightened Ones. They awakened by hearing the Buddha's sermons and contemplating these Twelve Conditioned Links. Those who attain the level of a Pratyekabuddha by contemplating these Twelve Conditioned Links when there is no Buddha in the world are known as Solitarily Enlightened Ones.

9. The Bodhisattva's Path to Buddhahood

Bodhisattvas are the trademark of Mahayana Buddhism. A Bodhisattva is an enlightened being who makes vast vows to rescue all living beings and guide them out of their suffering, to the bliss of Nirvana.

As we have seen, Hinayana practitioners are satisfied once they reach the level of an Arhat or Pratyekabuddha, whereas those who cultivate Mahayana diligently continue their practice until they can see their True Nature and break through to the level of a Bodhisattva. For the Mahayana practitioner, becoming a Bodhisattva is the first level that qualifies as enlightenment.

The initial level of enlightenment, where Bodhisattvas first get a clear look at their True Nature, is known as the First Ground. In all, there are Ten Grounds through which Bodhisattvas progress as they tirelessly strive to perfect their understanding. After they reach the Tenth Ground, Bodhisattvas can attain the level of Equal Enlightenment, which is followed by the Perfect Enlightenment of the Buddhas. In Sanskrit, the Buddha's level of enlightenment is known as Anuttara-Samyak-Sambodhi, which means "Unsurpassed Proper Equal Enlightenment."

Because the Buddha's level of understanding is incredibly difficult to attain, the Bodhisattva path spans many lifetimes, and enlightenment is necessarily a multi-lifetime process. It is not easy, and it takes a long time. The Bodhisattva's practice can be likened to polishing a mirror that is layered in dirt and grime. The more layers of dirt there are, the longer it takes to polish.

Only when they manage to completely polish the entire surface of the mirror, so that it can reflect all things perfectly without any distortions, will they have reached the state of a Buddha.

The Bodhisattva path starts with a single thought, which is known as the Bodhi resolve. This thought is simply the vow to attain the Perfect Enlightenment of a Buddha, no matter how many lifetimes it takes. One who sincerely makes this vow is said to have brought forth the Bodhi Mind, or Bodhicitta.

The spirit of the Bodhi Mind is captured by the Four Vast Vows of a Bodhisattva:

1. I vow to save the boundless living beings
2. I vow to sever the inexhaustible afflictions
3. I vow to study the countless Dharma Doors
4. I vow to accomplish the Unsurpassed Buddha Way.

Earth Store Bodhisattva, one of the major Bodhisattvas of Mahayana, exemplifies the first of these vows. Earth Store Bodhisattva is a translation of the Sanskrit name Ksitigharba, known as *Dì Zàng Pú Sà* 地藏菩薩 in Chinese. During one of his prior lifetimes, Earth Store Bodhisattva was a young woman who sincerely requested of the Buddhas to know the fate of her deceased mother. The woman then had a vision and experienced her mother to be suffering in the hells. She was so distraught that she vowed to attain enlightenment and save all living beings who fall to the hells. As a result, that woman cultivated and eventually became Earth Store Bodhisattva, and expressed her initial vow as follows: "If the hells are not empty I will not become a Buddha; only when living beings are all saved, will I attain Bodhi."

In other words, until there are no more beings suffering in the hells, Earth Store Bodhisattva will not rest in the final bliss of the Buddha's Nirvana, but rather will continue to be reborn, lifetime after lifetime, to rescue countless living beings. However, the hells will never be empty, and there will always be more living beings who need to be rescued. Thus, Earth Store Bodhisattva's vows are endless.

To some people, making such infinite vows, which are logically speaking impossible to accomplish, seems nonsensical. However, this is because we cannot understand the state of a Bodhisattva. In other words, since enlightenment cannot be grasped with our discriminating mind, it is foolish to try and rationally analyze the Four Vast Vows of a Bodhisattva.

Just know that the vow to save all living beings means that Bodhisattvas save everyone without discrimination, whether male or female, Chinese or Hispanic, animal or human, etc. That's how vast and expansive their mindset is.

Why do Bodhisattvas wish to save all beings in this way? Because they recognize that even animals like fish or small insects may have been our relatives in the past, and may be so again in the future. As I was once told at a large company where I used to work, it is wisest to treat everyone kindly because, "You never know who you will be working for next."

By benefiting all living beings without discrimination, Bodhisattvas create many affinities, or karmic connections, with living beings. When they then encounter these beings again in future lives, they will be able to use those affinities to teach and transform them.

Finally, we can look at these vast vows as follows: When the Bodhisattva's mind becomes truly endless, like the number of living beings that she has vowed to rescue, the Bodhisattva will instantly become a Buddha.

Without trying to understand these states with our thinking mind, we should instead have faith. If we too can make such vast vows, then one day we will understand for ourselves what it means to save all living beings and accomplish the Buddha Way.

Another great bodhisattva in Mahayana is Avalokiteśvara, the bodhisattva of compassion. In Chinese Buddhism, Avalokiteśvara is known as *Guān Yīn Pú Sà* 觀音菩薩. Like Earth Store Bodhisattva, Guan Yin has also made vast vows in the past. In particular, Guan Yin vowed to help those who are in danger or distress. Many Buddhists find that they get protection from Guan Yin by reciting her name in times of difficulty.

The story of Guan Yin's enlightenment through the Dharma Door of listening to her own Self Nature is recounted in the Shurangama Sutra. We will discuss this very effective method taught by Guan Yin in Chapter 33 of this book, where we will explain the basic techniques of Pure Land practice.

But for now, let us look at the Six Paramitas, which are practices that all Bodhisattvas use as they refine their understanding.

Paramita is a Sanskrit term meaning "to reach the other shore" or "to accomplish." Those who aspire to follow the Bodhisattva path are encouraged to practice these Dharmas to perfection.

The Six Paramitas are:

1. Giving: We can practice the giving of wealth, of Dharma and Fearlessness. External wealth includes money or material things, while inner wealth refers to the giving of body parts, such as organ donations. The giving of Dharma involves speaking Dharma for others, in order to help them attain liberation. The giving of fearlessness helps to allay fear and anxiety in others, when they arise. Of all three forms of giving, the giving of Dharma is foremost because it generates "non-outflow blessings." These are the kind of blessings necessary to reach Buddhahood, and will be further explained in Chapter 35, "The Currency of Blessings."

2. Precepts: These are the Buddhist rules of morality, clearly delineating right from wrong, good from evil. One could look at precepts as shields to provide protection against harm. When rules of morality are violated, we inevitably condemn ourselves to future retributions for our offenses. One can also look at precepts as a roadmap. By studying precepts, we learn to recognize danger and avoid cliffs and quagmires, so that our journey to Buddhahood is less perilous.

3. Patience: Cultivating patience requires enduring what cannot be endured. For example, we must pass the test of being yelled at for no reason, and yet not becoming afflicted. Or perhaps, we must endure

hunger and thirst as part of the test. The objective is to endure it all, until we can perfect our patience and reach a state called the Patience of Non-Production. At that point, there is nothing that we cannot endure.

4. Vigor: We practice vigor by relentlessly applying our effort in the following four ways:

    - We diligently strive to prevent potential evil from arising.
    - We apply ourselves to eliminating the evil that already exists.
    - We work hard to create all the potential good that has not yet arisen.
    - We earnestly nurture the good that has arisen so it will continue to grow.

5. Samadhi: Sanskrit for proper concentration, samadhi refers to the ability to sustain our concentration on the task at hand. Sustained concentration enables us to harness the power necessary to pierce through the fog of ignorance. This feature of samadhi is captured by the phrase "laser-like concentration," commonly known as mental strength. The Buddha taught that, "Restraining one's mind in one place, there is nothing that cannot be accomplished." In other words, to succeed in anything, we need to sustain our concentration, without distraction from externals, until the task is complete. One of the most effective methods to develop samadhi power, is by practicing Chan meditation.

6. Wisdom: Transcendental wisdom, or Prajna Wisdom, is the wisdom of the Mahayana sages: the

Buddhas and Bodhisattvas. In Mahayana, one is considered to have wisdom once one reaches enlightenment and is able to see True Emptiness. Then one is in touch with the Real Truth.

While the major Mahayana Dharma centers on the Six Paramitas, we are also encouraged to practice the Ten Thousand Aiding Practices. These practices include additional Dharma Doors such as bowing in repentance, reciting sutras, upholding mantras, explaining the Dharma, etc. The Ten Thousand Aiding Practices facilitate the perfection of the Six Paramitas.

By practicing these Six Paramitas and Ten Thousand Aiding Practices, Bodhisattvas gradually perfect their path to Buddhahood. In fact, in time we will all cultivate these Six Paramitas. Why is this? Because these Paramitas are the main path to Buddhahood, and Mahayana teaches that, eventually, each one of us will become a Buddha, with the same realization as Shakyamuni himself. It is just a matter of time.

However, the timescale involved here is enormous. It could take us millions, or even billions, of lifetimes to become a fully awakened Buddha.

In case you are wondering if there is a faster way, the answer, fortunately, is "Yes."

II

Introduction to Pure Land Buddhism

10. What is Pure Land Buddhism?

Life in this world is a constant struggle.

The Buddha found a solution, and taught us how we too can end the cycle of birth and death, free ourselves from all suffering and attain enlightenment. Ultimately, our aim is to realize the perfect state of a Buddha, so that we can one day teach and transform as many living beings as Shakyamuni Buddha himself has done in our world.

However, the path to accomplish Buddhahood is incredibly long and arduous, and spans many lifetimes. And every time we die and change to a new body, we face the risk of falling to the lower realms of rebirth, where we would experience great suffering, and regress from our goal of reaching perfect enlightenment.

That's why Pure Land Buddhism advocates seeking rebirth to the Pure Lands, where we can avoid the perils of reincarnation, and rapidly accelerate our progress toward enlightenment and toward attaining the Buddha's wisdom. The Pure Lands really are the best place for us because they offer the easiest and most direct path to enlightenment.

The Pure Lands are wonderful because life there is filled only with bliss, and the lifespan is incredibly long. But more importantly, all those who reach the Pure Lands are assured of attaining enlightenment by the end of their lifetime. Since those who are enlightened will never again return to the wheel of reincarnation, the Pure Lands offer a permanent escape from suffering.

The best-known Pure Land is the Western Bliss Pure Land, which we will often refer to simply as "The Pure Land." In Sanskrit, the Western Bliss Pure Land is known as Sukhāvatī, and in Chinese it is referred to as *Jílè* 極樂 ("Ultimate Bliss"), *Ānlè* 安樂 ("Peaceful Bliss"), or *Xītiān* 西天 ("Western Heaven"). Home to Amitabha Buddha and countless other enlightened sages, the Western Bliss Pure Land exists in a galaxy very far from ours. If we cultivate the methods of Pure Land Buddhism, we can be reborn in the Pure Land in our next lifetime, where we will be able to cultivate with Amitabha Buddha and the other enlightened sages who reside there.

Two great Bodhisattvas also serve as leaders of the Western Bliss Pure Land, alongside Amitabha. These are Guan Yin Bodhisattva and Great Strength Bodhisattva. Together, these three are known as the Three Worthy Ones, or the Three Sages (of the Western Bliss Pure Land).

If you visit a Pure Land temple, you will most likely see these Three Sages on the main altar. At the center is Amitabha Buddha; to his left stands Guan Yin Bodhisattva holding the pure vase, and to his right stands Great Strength Bodhisattva holding a lotus flower in his left hand.

Great Strength Bodhisattva, known in Chinese as *Dà Shì Zhì Pú Sà* 大勢至菩薩, or Mahāsthāmaprāpta in Sanskrit, became enlightened by reciting the Buddha's name. That is why he travels throughout our world teaching living beings to recite the Buddha's name in order to attain enlightenment or obtain rebirth to Amitabha's Pure Land.

The Western Bliss Pure Land of Amitabha, however, is only one example of a Pure Land. In fact, there are many Pure Lands in this Dharma Realm – which is a Buddhist term for the entire universe. Not only does the Dharma Realm contain countless Pure Lands, but it also contains countless other worlds like ours.

Generally, the different worlds throughout the Dharma Realm can be of two types:

- Defiled Lands, also known as Impure Lands
- Pure Lands

The world in which we live, referred to as the Saha world in Buddhism, is a perfect example of a defiled land. The Saha world is actually much bigger than our planet earth, and includes the entire Milky Way Galaxy.

What is the difference between Pure and Defiled Lands? The word defiled or impure says it all. Impure places are full of defilements. The inhabitants are confused and deluded. They commit evil acts, and rarely do good. They indulge in desire, fight and argue, take each other to court, cheat one another, and so forth. The Pure Lands, on the other hand, are very blissful places where cultivators gather to focus on goodness and attaining enlightenment. In addition, the entire physical environment in the Pure Lands is adorned by flowers, musical instruments, towering pavilions covered in gems, and other such appealing characteristics.

Just as Shakyamuni Buddha taught us about Amitabha's Western Bliss Pure Land, he also taught about the Vaidurya Pure Land of Medicine Master Buddha, another Pure Land that is located in the Eastern direction. In this Pure Land, there are both females and males, but there is no sexual desire. All inhabitants have the same adorned bodies as the Buddha's, meaning they share the 32 Hallmarks and 80 characteristics of the Buddha's body; these features are described in the sutras and include, for example, the Buddha's long ears, flat feet, and dark curly hair. The Vaidurya Pure Land is filled with superior cultivators such as Bodhisattvas, Pratyekabuddhas and Arhats. This Pure Land is just as adorned as Amitabha's Western Bliss Pure Land to the West.

Each world, whether pure or impure, is created by a Buddha in order to attract and serve certain types of living beings. Here we will use the terms "world" and "Buddhaland, or simply "Land," interchangeably.

As Bodhisattvas cultivate lifetime after lifetime on the long road to Buddhahood, they generate tremendous merit and virtue, which they then transfer toward the creation of their own Buddhaland. Once they become Buddhas, that land will become their home-base, from which they will teach and transform countless living beings. The Buddhaland can be created as they desire, possibly to reflect and honor those who assisted them in their prior cultivation.

For example, let's assume that you received help from the Indian people during the course of your cultivation to become a Buddha. You may choose to create a world that is comforting and familiar to those who helped you – for example a land with wonderful curries – so as to repay your debts to the people who helped you, and enable them to become Buddhas too. In this way, each Buddha creates a world upon accomplishing his cultivation.

You might wonder why Buddhas, who are enlightened, would create defiled worlds. Wouldn't it be more logical that they only create Pure Lands where everyone can be happy?

That would be nice. But let's think about it. If there are only Pure Lands, where can deluded people go?

In other words, Impure Lands are necessary to accommodate those who lack blessings, until they accrue enough good karma to make it to the Pure Lands.

Impure worlds are also ideal for Bodhisattvas and Buddhas to come and help living beings awaken to their suffering and experience what is known as "abhorrence" and "distancing:" In other words, those who are blessed will realize that the existence that most of us experience here in this world is not so desirable.

It takes wisdom and a lot of blessings to experience "abhorrence" and let go of our attachments to this existence. But once we do so, we will naturally want to "distance" ourselves from futile worldly pursuits, and resolve to be born to the Pure Lands where, from beginning to end, there is only bliss and absolutely no suffering.

For example, in our Saha world, many of us are preoccupied with material wealth and hoarding assets because, in our ignorance, we think that riches will bring us freedom and security. But becoming wealthy doesn't guarantee safety or freedom.

Those who reach the Pure Lands, however, will have true safety: they will never again fall into the lower realms to be reborn as ghosts, animals, or in the hells. Instead they will progress steadily toward enlightenment, the ultimate freedom.

Although Amitabha Buddha's Western Bliss Pure Land is only one of countless Pure Lands, as far as the residents of this Saha world are concerned, Amitabha's Pure Land represents our best chance of rebirth to a Pure Land. This is due to Amitabha Buddha's vow power and his great affinities with us.

11. Benefits of the Pure Land Approach

The Pure Land teachings, and Mahayana Buddhism in general, equip us with a new set of tools with which to tackle our problems. As we absorb the Mahayana perspective into our worldview, we will find more and more ways to improve ourselves and serve others. Our lives naturally will become more meaningful.

There are many ways that the Pure Land Dharma can help us improve. For instance, Pure Land practitioners have reported the following benefits:

1. Turning obstructions and difficulties into blessings
2. Fewer afflictions
3. Less stress
4. More peace of mind
5. A more pleasant lifestyle
6. Improved family life
7. Protection by the spirits, avoiding unexpected disasters and accidents
8. Increased wisdom
9. Becoming more compassionate and kind
10. A peaceful death, with less mental afflictions
11. Eradication of one's obstructions

Also, the Pure Land methods can improve our samadhi, or concentration power. This brings many benefits, from increased health and stamina, to relaxation and improved relationships with others. For more on how to build up your samadhi power, please see Chapters 33 and 37, as well as *The Chan Handbook: The Learner's Guide to Meditation*."

Also, knowing that there is more to life than the struggle and suffering we experience in our world today can be reassuring. After this life, things can get better, much better, if we practice well. Knowing this relieves some of the pressure from the suffering we currently face.

In particular, the Pure Land teachings are very effective at helping those who are extremely ill or dying. Such people usually do not have the time and energy that it would take to attain enlightenment and to resolve their karmic obstructions in this lifetime. However, because they are being forced to face the problem of suffering head-on, they can enter extremely focused and powerful states of mind. If they have faith in the Pure Land teachings, those who are sick can gain comfort by putting their illness in a broader, more meaningful, context. And some may even experience dramatic improvements to their health. Finally, those who are dying often are able to face death with much greater ease and peace.

This is illustrated in the following famous story that is noted in the "Records of Rebirths to the Western Bliss Pure Land 淨土往生錄:" Once, there was a butcher who specialized in selling beef. Toward the end of his life, he often dreamt of multitudes of cattle coming to harass him. He asked his wife to ask for help from the Buddhist sangha, or monastic community. A senior monk was called, who came and told them that the butcher's killing karma was very heavy: only reciting the Buddha's name could help. The butcher recited along with the monk. After a while, the (cattle) ghosts left and he felt a great sense of peace. As a result of this experience, the butcher came to have great faith in Amitabha and the Western Bliss Pure Land. Realizing that he had the opportunity to go to a much better place after his death, he continued to recite more earnestly. In a short time, he proclaimed that he saw the Buddha coming to greet him. He was reborn in the Western Bliss Pure Land.

In addition, we have had several instances where members of our temple have had dreams of their deceased relatives undergoing great suffering. When these people used special ceremonies that are available in Pure Land Buddhism to help the deceased, they later had dreams in which those relatives were doing well and had reached a much better place.

Ultimately, the suffering that we experience in this world is unnecessary and we can put an end to it. This is exactly what all of us should aspire to do. Those who are very sick or dying often have the impetus to recognize this faster than those who are healthy and doing well, and may thus be able to immediately resolve the problem by making it to the Western Bliss Pure Land after their death.

However, one need not be in crisis to benefit from the Pure Land Dharma Door. As we have seen, the Pure Land methods are especially suited for anyone unable to achieve enlightenment in this lifetime, which is most of us. The Pure Land Dharma Door has the unique advantage that it can be practiced by people of all abilities, from beginning to advanced. While some Pure Land practices are simple yet effective, others are much more subtle and difficult to understand and practice.

Those who take an intellectual approach to the teachings sometimes misinterpret the Pure Land Dharma Door as merely a story or an expedient device designed to motivate us to practice. However, this is a mistake that should be avoided: The Pure Lands really exist, just like our world.

If we make it to one of these Pure Lands, not only will we experience no suffering, but our existence will also be intrinsically meaningful. Instead of directing our energy toward worldly pursuits as we do in the Impure Lands, we will only have one thing to do: cultivate until we become Buddhas ourselves.

That is true happiness. That is security. That brings meaning to life.

12. Amitabha Buddha & His Forty Eight Vows

We have access to the Western Bliss Pure Land today, thanks to the past vows and practices of Amitabha Buddha.

In *The Amitabha Sutra*, Shakyamuni Buddha states: "Shariputra, what do you think? Why is this Buddha called Amitabha? Shariputra, the brilliance of that Buddha's light is measureless, illumining the Lands of the ten directions everywhere without obstruction, for this reason he is called Amitabha."

In fact, Amitabha's name means "limitless light." His light reaches everywhere. Thus all living beings can draw on his guidance and support.

Seeing how difficult it is for living beings to attain enlightenment and ultimately become Buddhas, Amitabha created a special Dharma to help us obtain rebirth to his Pure Land. He painstakingly cultivated to perfect his ability to help us attain rebirth. Then he invested the merit and virtue from his many lifetimes of cultivation toward the creation of the Western Bliss Pure Land. Now that his compassionate vows have been completed, his Pure Land has become one of the most ideal places imaginable for sincere cultivators to gather and be supported on their path.

Amitabha spent so long cultivating the Bodhisattva path, that he has affinities with vast numbers of living beings throughout the Universe. Thanks to Amitabha's vows, all we have to do now is recite his name, and we can immediately draw on his power to help us make progress.

Even among the blessed, Amitabha shines.

How did Amitabha ever create such a powerful method of helping living beings?

Long ago, in a former lifetime, Amitabha Buddha was a powerful king. This king repeatedly made offerings to World Self-Mastery King Buddha, a previous Buddha from the distant past. After making offerings, the king listened to this Buddha speak Dharma. Later, the king gave up his throne, left the home-life, and became known as Dharma Treasury Bhikshu (Bhikshu is Sanskrit for a male monastic or "left-home person").

While cultivating the Way[3], Dharma Treasury Bhikshu asked World Self-Mastery King Buddha to show him the best worlds in the Dharma Realm. The Buddha used his spiritual powers to reveal all the worlds, and even explained to Dharma Treasury Bhikshu how each one was created.

---

[3] "Cultivating the Way" is a Buddhist expression that technically refers to the practice of the Four Noble Truths, discussed in Chapter 8. However, it also can refer in a general sense to cultivating any of the Buddha's methods for reaching enlightenment.

Dharma Treasury Bhikshu then resolved, through his cultivation, to create the best possible Pure Land. Thus he made 48 great vows. These vows propelled him toward eventually, in the distant future, attaining perfect enlightenment and becoming Amitabha Buddha.

For instance, in one of his vows, Dharma Treasury Bhikshu states that: “I will not become a Buddha until I have created a world where all beings who single-mindedly recite my name 10 times will be reborn.”

Further, Dharma Treasury Bhikshu vowed that he would not become a Buddha until he had created a land where living beings would no longer have to suffer, and would progress steadily towards Buddhahood. Yes: in the Pure Land, you can become a Buddha in one lifetime, without ever again returning to the wheel of reincarnation.

In each of his 48 great vows, Dharma Treasury Bhikshu says that he refuses to become a Buddha unless all of these 48 vows come true.

Dharma Treasury Bhikshu subsequently cultivated for countless lifetimes to fulfill these vows. Ten great kalpas ago, his cultivation was successful and he reached perfect enlightenment; thus he became Amitabha Buddha. This means that all of Amitabha’s 48 vows have been fulfilled for more than 10 great kalpas (which is an incredibly long time). Thus all the techniques that Amitabha conceived of in each of these vows, are now manifest and ready for us to use.

Amitabha cultivated as a Bodhisattva for so long, that he generated enough merit and karmic affinities to create a world that beings from all over the universe can now use as a way-station to enlightenment. That was how the Western

Bliss Pure Land was created. This is well documented in the Small and Large Amitabha Sutras.

Once we reach the Pure Land, we will have Amitabha Buddha himself as our teacher, and thus will have a much easier time realizing the profound principles of Buddhism.

While it is most desirable to go to the Pure Lands – any will do – this is not easy to accomplish. We should know that we can go to any Pure Land of our choice. However, in this world we have such strong affinities with Amitabha Buddha that his Western Bliss Pure Land is the easiest one for us to reach. Thus, all the Buddhas praise Amitabha Buddha and countless great Bodhisattvas themselves vow to obtain rebirth there.

Since even the Bodhisattvas resolve to go to the Pure Lands to cultivate, we should follow suit and do so as well.

13. A Day of Life in the Pure Land

To find out what Western Bliss Pure Land is like, we can consult *The Buddha Speaks of Amitabha Sutra*. In this sutra, also known as *The Small Amitabha Sutra* or simply *The Amitabha Sutra*, Shakyamuni Buddha describes the Pure Land, saying:

"Shariputra, in that Buddhaland when the soft wind blows, the rows of jeweled trees and jeweled nets give forth subtle and wonderful sounds, like one hundred thousand kinds of music played at the same time. All those who hear these sounds naturally bring forth in their hearts mindfulness of the Buddha, mindfulness of the Dharma, and mindfulness of the Sangha."

This sutra contains many more descriptions of the unsurpassed adornments and bliss that are found in the Pure Land: everything about the environment there, from the trees and pavilions, to all the inhabitants, and the Buddhas and Bodhisattvas who act as teachers, everything helps us practice the Dharma and aids us in understanding the profound meaning of the Buddha's teachings.

And of course, there is absolutely no suffering in Western Bliss Pure Land. You cannot imagine a more wonderful life than you'll experience there. When you wake up in the morning, you can see the pools of multicolored lotuses that stretch out before your palace. Or, if you live in one of the palaces that are suspended in the sky, your morning meditation may be accompanied by the light illuminating the clouds all around you, and reflecting in the seven precious gems that adorn your palace.

After your meditation, you may decide to go for a swim in the pools of water with eight virtuous qualities or go for a stroll – all the while, the sound of the birds singing in the crisp morning air, the sublime music of the wind passing through the trees, the golden glow of the earth beneath your feet: everything fills you with a profound sense of wonder and joy at the depth of the Buddha's teachings and wisdom.

In the Saha world, your sense perceptions used to fuel your desires and distract you from cultivation. But in Pure Land, everything that you perceive and experience increases your concentration and helps you unfold your inherent wisdom. As you walk back home, breathing in the delicate fragrance of lotus blossoms, you may contemplate your gratitude to Amitabha Buddha for creating such a wonderful world, where the whole environment speaks Dharma and supports your cultivation.

Finishing your walk, you gather some flowers for offerings. Since everyone in the Pure Land can make use of Amitabha's spiritual powers, you are able to travel freely anywhere throughout the entire universe. Every day before the midday meal, you visit distant worlds to pay your respects and learn from other Buddhas there.

When you return, it is time for your meal. Whatever food you desire appears, as you eat in mindfulness. After you finish, you may sit with your fellow cultivators and discuss finer points of the Dharma.

In the afternoon, you might bathe in the lotus pools, which adjust their temperature to your liking, and nourish your good roots – i.e. the great blessings that give you the potential to progress in your cultivation.

The water that flows into the pools speaks the Dharma of suffering, impermanence, no-self and emptiness. You appreciate how every moment of your life is devoted to cultivation. There is no need to work or earn money. You have no illnesses, addictions, or obstructions. The three lower paths of the animals, ghosts and hells do not even exist in the Western Bliss Pure Land, so there are no ghosts or demons to harass you.

In the evening, after some more meditation or sutra study, Guan Yin Bodhisattva may give a Dharma Talk. Or possibly Amitabha Buddha himself will speak for the assembly in his Dharma Hall on top of a pavilion made of the seven precious metals and gems: gold, silver, lapis lazuli, crystal, mother-of pearl, red pearls and carnelian. After the lecture, you may wish to finish the day with some more meditation, so that you can absorb the new Dharma that you have just heard.

Every day, your cultivation reveals new facets of the Buddha's wisdom; you constantly develop insights, as you progress through the stages of Arhatship and ascend through the levels of the Bodhisattva Path. Day by day, you see your Buddha Nature with greater and greater clarity, and learn to appreciate the infinite subtlety of your own True Mind.

You are free from fear, as you know that you will live like this for many aeons, until you eventually perfect your enlightenment. Then you will be able to return to the Impure Lands, only this time as a Buddha, at which time you will cross over countless living beings from the shore of suffering, to the other shore of Nirvana.

Truly, who could ask for anything more?

III

Essential Concepts of Pure Land Buddhism

14. The Best Dharma Door

The Buddha provides many entry points through which living beings can enter his world. If we can pass through these Dharma Doors, we can then attain the Buddha's knowledge.

Dharma Doors refer to the various methods of Buddhist practices. Buddhas and Bodhisattvas come to our world to teach these methods to help us reach enlightenment.

When Shakyamuni Buddha brought Buddhism to the Saha world more than 2,500 years ago, he taught many different Dharma Doors, all of which are very powerful. However, there is one Dharma Door that is particularly suited to the present time. That Dharma Door is Pure Land Buddhism.

To see why, we can look to the three major periods of Buddhism:

The Proper Dharma Era: This period took place during the first 500 years after the Buddha's Nirvana. During this time, the cultivation of Samadhi (concentration) through meditation was common, and people attained sagehood fairly easily.

The Dharma Semblance Era: During the next 500 years,

people preferred to cultivate blessings by building temples and images.

The Dharma Ending Era: We are currently in this era, in which the Buddha predicted the world would be filled with fighting and conflict and few people would earnestly cultivate the Dharma or strive to live virtuous lives.

Ever since we entered the Dharma ending era almost 2,000 years ago, Buddhism has gradually been declining, and continues its descent. According to the Buddha, this period will last for a total of 10,000 years, and at the end of this era, Buddhism will become extinct.

It is not difficult to see the signs of the Dharma Ending Era all around us: we live in an increasingly hectic and scattered culture that promotes self-indulgence and exalts the ego. Pressures to succeed and attain material comforts can overwhelm us, and leave little time and inclination to reach out and help others.

Thus it is more difficult to become enlightened in present day society than it was in the past. In fact, the majority of people who investigate and practice the Buddha's teachings today, will not be able to attain enlightenment in a single lifetime.

And even if one can reach the initial stages of enlightenment, it still takes so much more work to progress along the Bodhisattva path and eventually become a Buddha, which is the ultimate aim for all Mahayana practitioners.

The enormity of this undertaking explains why the overwhelming majority of us will fall short by the time we die. We will continue to revolve in the wheel of reincarnation, and if we are unprepared, we may end up falling to the lower realms of rebirth, which we certainly should avoid.

However, as we have seen, if we are reborn in the Western Bliss Pure Land we will avoid the risks and perils of reincarnation, because the conditions in the Pure Land are so supportive of cultivation that we will be assured of attaining enlightenment in that very lifetime. Once we accomplish enlightenment, then we will never again be blindly tossed about by the relentless cycle of birth and death.

Since we are currently in the Dharma Ending Era during which the teachings of Buddhism are becoming more rare, we are especially blessed to encounter Mahayana and its 84,000 Dharma Doors of practice. We must not forget the kindness of the patriarchs, who made it possible for us to receive these teachings today. The patriarchs are the lineage of enlightened masters, dating back to the time of the Buddha himself, who have been entrusted with the responsibility of passing the Proper Dharma on to the subsequent generations.

In particular, gratitude must be given to Great Master Xuan Hua, who founded *The City of Ten Thousand Buddhas* and *The Dharma Realm Buddhist Association.* He brought Mahayana from China to the United States, and lectured extensively on the Mahayana Sutras. The English translations of his teachings are among the best and most accurate records of the Mahayana Dharma available in English.

Since Great Master Xuan Hua is the latest known patriarch, everyone who wishes to learn the Proper Dharma is encouraged to draw near him and study his teachings.

Great Master Xuan Hua brought the five major Chinese schools of Buddhism to the United States:

1. The Vinaya School: They investigate the precepts and rules of conduct in order to build the necessary foundation for liberation.

2. The Teachings School: They research and extensively elaborate on the Buddhist principles in order to unfold wisdom.

3. The Chan School: They concentrate on meditation practices in order to become enlightened.

4. The Secret School: They hold tantras or mantras, which are prayers or chants that have special powers. For instance the Medicine Master Mantra can promote healing and improve health.

5. The Pure Land School: They recite the Buddha's name, hoping for rebirth to the Pure Lands.

There is another reason why Pure Land Buddhism is considered the "best" Dharma Door for our times: the single method of reciting the Buddha's name encompasses not only the Pure Land School, but the other Four Schools as well.

- By reciting the Buddha's name, one can end false-thinking and sever attachments: that is the Chan School.

- Amitabha Buddha's name contains countless meanings and principles: that is the Teaching School.

- Those with some skill can recite Buddha's name until they reach a profound state where all three karmas of body, mouth and mind are purified: that is the Vinaya School.

- The phrase "Amitabha" (or "Emituofo" in Chinese) can function as a mantra which has been known to chase ghosts away, resolve enmity, eradicate karmic retributions, help us get what we want and subdue demons: that is the Secret School.

In the past, one of the Pure Land patriarchs was asked for help when the area where he was cultivating suffered a year-long drought. He humbly said that he could not do much but recite the Buddha's name on their behalf. He hit a bell as he walked around the affected area while loudly reciting the Buddha's name. It rained wherever he went.

Practitioners of all the Five Schools of Buddhism often ask what Dharma Door they should practice. The answer is Pure Land Buddhism, because it has been demonstrated that many advanced practitioners have accomplished their Dharma with the recitation of the Buddha's name.

All Dharma Doors, from any of the five schools of Buddhism, are designed to develop samadhi, or concentration power. Pure Land Buddhism can also effectively develop samadhi power, just like many other methods. But if there are many ways to cultivate samadhi, why are Pure Land methods the "best?"

It is because the Pure Land Dharma Door can accommodate a wide range of practitioners: from those with superior roots to those with dull roots. Here "superior roots" refers to those few people who are very blessed and have most likely been practicing Mahayana for many lifetimes already, whereas "dull roots" refers to those who have a harder time understanding the Dharma, and had minimal exposure to the Dharma in previous lifetimes. In other words, the Pure Land methods are appropriate for people of all levels and capacities.

Those with superior roots are not above the techniques of the Pure Land School. In fact, even many high-level practitioners such as the Tenth Ground Bodhisattvas specialize in reciting the Buddha's name. Those with superior roots already understand that to recite Amitabha is to recite all the Buddhas' names, and to be reborn to the Western Bliss Pure Land is to be reborn to all Buddhalands of the ten directions.

Those with shallow roots, on the other hand, can simply recite the Buddha's name to obtain rebirth and escape suffering.

Since the practice of Chan is very difficult to accomplish, it is typically best suited for those with superior roots. But when practiced together with Chan, the Pure Land teachings can make Chan accessible to a wider range of people.

Further, the Chan School has Dharma Doors that are very powerful for developing samadhi; thus Pure Land practitioners can use Chan tools to develop their skills more quickly.

Finally, and most importantly, we cultivate in order to help others. And Pure Land Buddhism provides effective methods for doing just this.

How can we use Pure Land methods to help others?

First, by not allowing ourselves to become a burden to others: we should strive to save ourselves first in order to avoid inflicting our confusion on others and being a liability to society.

Also, we can help save other people by utilizing the many tools that Pure Land Buddhism has developed for helping others obtain rebirth, so that they too will experience only bliss and no longer experience suffering.

Finally, when we reach the Pure Land, we will cultivate until we perfect our wisdom. Then we will each be able to return to the defiled worlds as a Buddha, and save countless living beings.

That is the spirit of great compassion in Mahayana. We save ourselves in order to be able to save others. We then learn to save others in order to perfect saving ourselves.

The style of practicing Chan and Pure Land in parallel, which we have been discussing here, originates from the teachings of Great Master Xuan Hua. To learn more about the parallel practice of Chan and Pure Land, see Part VI: "Chan and Pure Land Parallel Practice: A How To Guide."

15. Only Bliss

In general, worldly happiness represents the fulfillment of our human desires of the senses. For example, we are happy when we enjoy a delicious meal, are praised, listen to beautiful music, or feel loved. There may be deeper levels of happiness, but these, too, are considered worldly.

The wise Buddhist distinguishes between "happiness" and "bliss." The happiness that we typically experience from our sense pleasures is rather coarse. In contrast, bliss represents a more refined type of happiness, such as is experienced in the heavenly realms.

For example, in the Desire Realm heavens, the gods and goddesses experience bliss, and not merely happiness. The heavenly beings also experience sensual love that is much deeper, and more wonderful, than sensual love in the human realm.

In some heavens, the gods wear heavenly garments which are much more refined than the best garments in the human realm. These garments are perfectly fitted to each heavenly dweller and will never get dirty and therefore require no washing. They appear exactly as one wishes; such is the nature of their heavenly blessings. The same applies to other material things relating to the rest of the senses.

There are two types of heavenly bliss:

1. That which comes from blessings, as is the case for the heavenly beings in the six Desire Heavens.

2. That which comes from samadhi power which generates a very refined type of bliss. The higher the samadhi level, the higher the level of bliss.

Just like everything else, bliss is also limited in duration. For example, in the highest heaven of the Triple Realm, the Heaven of Neither Thought Nor Non-Thought, the lifespan is 80,000 great kalpas. This is an incredibly long time period, as one great kalpa lasts over a billion years. Although the inhabitants of this heaven experience tremendous bliss for so long, they will eventually experience suffering at the end of their heavenly lifespan when they fall back onto the wheel of reincarnation.

Similarly, the residents of the Western Bliss Pure Land also experience bliss that is considerably more refined than that which is experienced in Impure Lands like our Saha world. That Pure Land is also known as the Land of Utmost Bliss because the bliss that is experienced by its residents is unsurpassed in all of the Dharma Realm. It is so much better than anything we can conceive of in our world.

Furthermore, those in the Pure Land will be in the company of the most enlightened people. They are so much more pleasant to be around. We can greatly benefit from these enlightened beings' wisdom light. Such is the nature of one's existence in that Pure Land until the end of one's life there.

Yes, the inhabitants of the Pure Land also have a limited lifespan. However, their lifespan is much longer, and their conditions are so conducive to cultivating, that they will become a Buddha in one lifetime and never have to return to the wheel of reincarnation.

Those who make it to the Western Bliss Pure Land will permanently put an end to all sorts of suffering: no more addiction to food, drugs or alcohol, no more problems with in-laws, no more bosses, and no more of life's struggles—ever!

All of this makes cultivating a supremely worthwhile endeavor. But the question remains: How do we get there?

16. Only Ten Recitations

In *The Buddha Speaks of Amitabha Sutra*, also known as *The Small Amitabha Sutra*, it is said that if we can manage to recite Amitabha Buddha's name 10 times "with one mind unconfused" then at the end of our lives, Amitabha Buddha himself and the assembly of sagely ones from the Western Bliss Pure Land will come to greet us and bring us back to the Pure Land with them.

It may sound easy but it is, in fact, more complicated. Not only is the Buddha's help in reaching the Western Bliss Pure Land essential, but the Buddha must also agree to help us obtain rebirth to his land.

So, what do we need to do exactly?

We only need to recite his name 10 times in a row, "with one mind unconfused." The state of having "one mind unconfused" is also known as the Buddha Recitation Samadhi.

The technical details of this samadhi are beyond the scope of this introductory book. But generally speaking, we must be able to recite his name 10 times in succession, without a single intervening thought in between.

Students who have reached respectable levels of samadhi (fourth Dhyana and higher) may believe that they are capable of reciting the Buddha's name without intervening thoughts; but in actuality, at this level their minds are still coarse, and full of false-thinking.

In the state of reciting the Buddha's name "with one mind unconfused," one holds the Buddha's name in the mind without forgetting, to the point where no other thought arises. The Buddha's name follows in thought after thought, without interruption from any other thought. That is true discipline!

Entering this level of samadhi is so difficult that many advanced practitioners, who have devoted their entire lives to reciting the Buddha's name every day for decades, have only been able to enter this samadhi a few times in their entire lives.

Clearly, it is not easy to enter the Buddha Recitation Samadhi, but it is not impossible. Why not? For one thing, there are many more samadhi levels in Buddhism that are much higher.

Those who believe they can enter this level of samadhi should confirm it with a wise teacher. He or she will be able to confirm whether you have really accomplished this level, because there is something wonderful that happens when you enter this samadhi. This is a Buddhist secret that cannot be casually divulged.

Most Pure Land practitioners don't realize that it is very difficult to enter the Buddha Recitation Samadhi without a wise teacher. They seem to believe that they can obtain rebirth by simply reciting the Buddha's name. This could not be further from the truth. Only those who reach the Buddha recitation samadhi, can have this kind of assurance, because Amitabha Buddha will know about their intentions and will aid them at the time of death.

But how does Amitabha Buddha know about our intentions? What will make us stand out from the countless beings who aspire for rebirth to his land?

As we mentioned, Amitabha Buddha does not know about us until his name is recited 10 times "with one mind unconfused." If we can manage to do this, then it is tantamount to sending a telegram to Amitabha, telling him of our sincere wish to go to his land. Then we can get on the list of those to be ferried to the Pure Land upon our death.

All we have to do to ensure our own rebirth is to enter this recitation samadhi, and we only have to do it once to get on the passenger list.

There are some who think that they must do the recitation at the time of death; this is not so.

Moreover, there are some who think that they can simply live a worldly life and wait until the time of death to start reciting the Buddha's name. This is the same as thinking that you can easily hit a hole in one the very first time you play golf!

This is why we typically organize training sessions to teach the Buddha recitation techniques. Our followers regularly come to the temple on the weekend to practice. They even participate in the week-long recitation sessions called "Fo Qi," Chinese for Buddha Seven, meaning we recite the Buddha's name for seven days.

Our access to the Western Bliss Pure Land must be earned.

It is hard work; but the results are profound.

17. Too Good To Be True

The Pure Land Dharma Door is a wonderful and highly effective method. However, one must be on the lookout for those who make exaggerated and false claims.

For instance, one of my disciples told me that her relative asked her to watch another monk's DVD on Pure Land Buddhism. That monk guarantees that anyone who watches his DVD will be reborn to the Western Bliss Pure Land at the time of death.

If it were that easy to obtain rebirth to the Pure Land, then why bother reciting the Buddha's name? Amitabha Buddha himself says that we must be able to recite his name 10 times with one mind unconfused before he will come and bring us back to his Buddhaland upon our death. And, as has been noted previously, the state of reciting with "one mind unconfused" is incredibly difficult to attain.

Traditional Mahayana practice requires that we must earn every good thing that happens to us. The basic law of karma requires that rewards and blessings must be earned; we also need to earn our place in Buddhism.

For example, when the Buddha speaks Dharma to the Great Assembly, the Bodhisattvas and Arhats generally get to sit while the rest of the Dharma protectors must stand. This reflects stature within the community that was earned by their prior contributions.

Ultimately, we cannot become Buddhas and Bodhisattvas unless we work for it. No wise teacher would encourage their followers by promising shortcuts, giving guarantees or condoning laziness. Buddhism is an equitable meritocracy.

Wise teachers are often called Good Knowing Advisers in Buddhism. They invariably encourage their pupils to work hard. More often than not, they speak of things that are difficult to hear. Why? Their teachings are designed to minimize the enormous self, and not to aggrandize it. Therefore their teachings are threatening to the ego, and can be hard to accept.

This is the part that is hard for us confused people to accept. The teacher's job is to point out our flaws. If we are sincere, then they can teach us how to go about fixing them.

What sacrifices have you made to prove your sincerity? If you have done nothing for Mahayana, then don't expect the Buddha to help you.

Good Knowing Advisers teach their students to guard against their own greedy minds, and not believe in guarantees and empty promises. If obtaining rebirth to the Pure Land were that easy, then the Bodhisattvas would not be necessary.

For those who work hard and apply the right methods, rebirth to the Pure Land is not too good to be true. If one can accomplish the Pure Land Dharma Door, then the suffering one experiences in this lifetime is the very last suffering one will ever have to undergo.

Those who make it to the Pure Land at the time of their death, will never again have to worry about finding a job, having enough to eat, getting sick, or dying. Neither will they have to worry about ever again falling to the hells, or becoming a ghost or an animal.

It may be hard work to cultivate the Pure Land Dharma, but the benefits are well worth it!

18. Horizontal Escape

It is very difficult to attain enlightenment. The sutras tell us that, in the Dharma Ending Age that we are in, for every million people who practice Chan, only one will succeed in awakening.

However, one should not despair at these figures. Rather, it should be considered a blessing to have encountered the Pure Land Dharma Door, of which the ancients said, "For every ten thousand who recite the Buddha's name, ten thousand will be reborn to the Pure Land."

Yes, this Dharma Door really is that powerful. However, this statement should be qualified: what it is really telling us is that everyone who recites the Buddha's name will make it to the Pure Land *eventually*, though it could still take many, many more lifetimes. However, for those who wish to ensure that they will make it to the Pure Land in their *very next* lifetime, then the odds again become more challenging. But the odds are still much more favorable than if Chan were practiced alone.

To compare the approaches of Chan and Pure Land, consider the following analogy: imagine a tall stalk of bamboo with a worm trapped inside of it. The worm is down at the very bottom of the bamboo and wishes to get up to the top, which symbolizes attaining Bodhi, or awakening. Succeeding at Chan practice can be likened to the worm climbing vertically up to the top of the bamboo, by crawling along the inside of the bamboo stalk and successively eating its way through each of the partitions that divide the many segments of the stalk. Every segment that the worm must eat through is analogous to the levels of difficulty which Chan practitioners face both in increasing their samadhi power, and in using this samadhi power to break through all the negative karma that they have been accumulating since the beginning of time.

Indeed, Chan practitioners must pass through many barriers. Just as the worm who wishes to climb up through the inside of the bamboo is in for quite a challenge, so too must the Chan practitioner summon extreme determination to single-handedly battle the 10,000 demons and even give up her life in the process, if need be.

Pure Land practice, however, is analogous to the worm eating its way horizontally out from inside the core of the bamboo stalk, and then crawling in an unimpeded fashion up the side of the bamboo until it reaches the top. Clearly, the worm that climbs up the outside of the bamboo will have a much easier time than the one inside, which must eat through segment after segment.

Similarly, the Pure Land practitioner who draws on Amitabha's vow power can bypass all the many karmic obstructions that the Chan practitioner must face head on. By drawing on Amitabha's vows to help all beings who have faith in him and recite his name, one can horizontally escape from the three realms of rebirth.

The analogy of the bamboo demonstrates the power of the Pure Land Dharma Door, which not only offers an easier, more secure, and faster path to attaining Buddhahood, but also takes the uncertainty out of rebirth.

19. Baggage for the Pure Land

At this point, the astute reader may ask: "If we can horizontally escape our karmic retributions and be reborn in the Pure Land, where we will only experience bliss, does this mean that we can escape the law of cause and effect?" In other words, if we reach the Pure Land, we will never have to suffer again. So what happens to all the retributions we were supposed to experience as a result of our past karma?

The Pure Land Dharma is not outside of the law of cause and effect. When we are reborn to the Pure Land, our past karma is not eradicated, but we actually carry it with us. This is called "carrying your karma with rebirth," and is also known as "bringing your baggage to the Pure Land," where baggage is an analogy for your retributions.

All of us have unsettled retributions, whether good or bad, that we have generated since beginningless time. Typically, our negative karma acts as a burden that causes suffering and obstructions in future lifetimes. However, we can break that cycle in Pure Land, where our retributions become inactive, and are "suspended" until they can later be settled.

It's like traveling to a foreign country and skipping town on all your creditors.

Once you begin your cultivation in the Pure Land, your

negative karma will be unable to manifest, and you will have the opportunity to work on your past offenses, without experiencing the kind of suffering that we do here in our world.

How is this possible? It is all thanks to Amitabha Buddha and the blissful environment he created in the Pure Land.

Imagine that: in the Pure Land, you will not have to experience the consequences of the evil karma you have committed in all your previous lives. In many cases, you will be able to gradually resolve your karmic obstructions, without ever having to part from the bliss that is available in the Pure Land.

In other cases you will eventually be able to use these karmic debts as a way to help others. For example, let's say that you owe your sister $2,000 but you died before you had the chance to repay her. If you are born to the Pure Land, you can bring that debt with you. Perhaps, once you are skilled enough you may then ask Amitabha for permission to return to the Saha land to repay her principal, with interest. After having trained in the Pure Land with Amitabha Buddha himself, imagine the kind of good you'll be able to do for her.

Some people, when they hear that it's possible to bring our karma with us to the Pure Land, often ask: "In that case, can bad people obtain rebirth?"

The straight answer is: "Yes, they can; and many have."

Even if we have made many mistakes and have heavy karma, as long as we meet the three requisites of Faith, Vows and Practice, then we can all go to the Pure Land. These three requisites will be discussed in Chapters 23 – 25.

Some strongly object to allowing bad people into the Pure Land, and find this to be unfair.

On the surface, this objection is understandable; but if you look more closely, maybe we can see why Amitabha, at times, welcomes even bad people to the Pure Land.

Imagine that one of your relatives is on death row and about to be executed. Even if he is guilty and is a bad man, wouldn't you still wish for him to reach the Pure Land, and leave behind all the suffering he had to endure in this defiled Saha world of ours? Hasn't he suffered enough and paid off his debts to society through his incarceration and execution?

Furthermore, what if he really is innocent, as he has always maintained, and as you believe? Wouldn't it be fair for him to start enjoying bliss, never again suffer, and always have meaning in his life?

What about those who are truly evil, and who got away with their destructive acts? Do they deserve a place in the Pure Land too?

But who are we to judge others? "Bad" is such a relative term. You may regard a man as evil, but don't you think his mother can still see some goodness in him?

I believe that it is how Amitabha feels about it.

Unlike us, he does not discriminate. He neither sees evil in people, nor does he see goodness in them: he only sees a future Buddha in all of us. He only wants to help us develop our true potential.

Furthermore, once evil people get to the Pure Land, they will change and become good. And good people will become even better, once they get to see Amitabha Buddha.

Instead of worrying about others and questioning Amitabha's wisdom in accepting bad people to the Pure Land, shouldn't we be more concerned about our own rebirth? In fact, shouldn't we be glad that Amitabha does not require us to be perfect, before letting us into his Pure Land?

When one of my disciples asked: "If I am bad, can I still get to the Pure Land?" I replied to her: "If you mean you have broken precepts, then yes, you can still have a chance reach the Pure Land at your time of death. Even if you repeatedly break precepts, you can still go to the Pure Land, provided you have enough rebirth blessings. But you should also remember that being bad will definitely hamper your chances to be reborn. The more often you break precepts, the more difficult it will be for you to obtain rebirth to the Western Bliss Pure Land."

My disciple then asked me how to create rebirth blessings.

I explained to her that if she aspires for rebirth to the Pure Land, it takes action, not just wishful thinking. She needs to do something about it. I advised her to recite the Buddha's name more fervently and invest in her own rebirth by going to a good temple and requesting help to generate even more rebirth blessings.

In conclusion, the Pure Land Dharma Door is wonderful in that it enables us to carry our baggage, our retributions for past offenses, to the Pure Land. There we will learn much more effective ways to resolve them and pay off our karmic debts. That is how compassionate and forgiving Amitabha is: he does not judge us and will give us a chance, if we are smart, to accrue enough blessings to obtain rebirth to his country.

Incidentally, though we are not yet in the Pure Land, it does not hurt for us emulate Amitabha, and learn to discriminate less and forgive more. Such is the spirit of great compassion found in the Pure Land Dharma Door.

20. Insurance Policy

Wise people buy insurance to protect themselves against catastrophes. Insurance policies are designed to provide protection against debilitating losses that are unlikely to happen.

In Buddhism, the moments of birth and death are dangerous phases of our existence. In particular, death can be most catastrophic if we fall into any of the three lower realms of the hells, the hungry ghosts or the animals. Without doubt, the hells are the worst place we could end up. And those who become hungry ghosts or animals, will be wretchedly unhappy. More importantly, falling to any of these destinations would be a catastrophic interruption of our spiritual journey.

If we recognize that the danger of falling into these lower realms is very real, then it is easy to see the value of the Pure Land Dharma Door. In fact, if we understand this Dharma Door and practice it correctly, it can be like an insurance policy that will protect us against these kinds of worst-case scenarios.

Since the chances of escaping from the hells anytime soon are practically nil, and the suffering that we will endure while there is overwhelming, it should be glaringly obvious that the hells are to be avoided at all costs.

Although it is not as bad as being in the hells, existence as a hungry ghost is unimaginably hard. Ghosts have a very long lifespan and are usually so miserable that they wish to die, but they cannot.

Even when ghosts die, they are usually reborn again for many consecutive lifetimes as ghosts before they finally pay off their karmic debts and rise to higher realms of rebirth.

After having undergone a sufficient amount of suffering, they may be reborn as animals. While better than becoming a ghost or going to the hells, becoming an animal is also an undesirable fate.

Therefore, just as savvy people buy insurance, astute cultivators buy Buddhist insurance.

Ideally, cultivators should acquire insurance for this life as well as for future lives, when they face the risk of falling into the wheel of reincarnation.

How can we do this?

Reciting the Buddha's name is the best insurance against potential catastrophes. The samadhi power we develop by reciting the Buddha's name is known as self-help.

In addition, when we recite his name, we also receive help from others: we receive the inconceivable benefits that come from Amitabha Buddha's name itself, due to his 48 great vows. Each recitation of the Buddha's name can eradicate countless past offenses that could otherwise cause us to fall into the three evil paths upon death. It therefore is a good insurance policy against falling this lifetime.

Furthermore, if you can recite the Buddha's name until you enter the Buddha Recitation Samadhi, you will be assured of rebirth to the Pure Land. Although this is not at all easy to do, it is the ultimate protection for future lives since it will enable us to permanently disengage from the wheel of reincarnation.

21. Irreversibility

The Pure Land Dharma Door is a supreme form of insurance. Why? Because all those who reach the Pure Land immediately attain irreversibility.

Irreversibility is also known as non-regression or non-retreating. The principle of non-regression is crucial for accomplishing your goals. If all your efforts move you toward your goal, and if you do not backtrack, then all you have to do is persevere, and eventually you will succeed.

Those who make it to the Pure Land will never have to worry about falling into the three evil paths *ever* again, because everyone in the Pure Land is an avaivartika; this is a Sanskrit word for the level at which you will no longer regress.

Typically, the process of cultivation is fraught with many ups and downs. New students initially get excited with the rapid progress they make. However, almost all of them will eventually experience regression.

For example, one disciple of mine was able to sit in full-lotus for three hours a day, for years. After reaching this most remarkable milestone in her 70s, she began complaining that she could barely sit for half an hour. That is regression. It is not uncommon for cultivators to take one step forward and immediately move back two steps. Such is the nature of cultivation in the Impure Lands.

In addition to the risk of regressing during our cultivation, we must also consider the risk of regression associated with the birth and death process. Even advanced cultivators such as Arhats or Bodhisattvas experience regression as they go through birth and death.

Arhats have the "confusion with dwelling in the womb" while Bodhisattvas have the "splitting the yin" confusion[4]. Unless they can meet with a Good Knowing Adviser, then life after life they retreat, and find it very hard to bring forth the Bodhi mind.

The bottom line is: at the time of death, it is very easy to regress. Since this is true for the sages, we can imagine how much greater the risk of regression at death is for ordinary people. If we fall to any of the three lower realms, we will most likely be stuck there and unable to cultivate for many lifetimes.

Fortunately, the Pure Land Dharma Door is especially designed to help us avoid regressing at the time of death, and ensure that we do not fall to the three lower realms.

Those who reach the Pure Land are guaranteed that they will continue to make progress in their cultivation, until they eventually reach Buddhahood. Their spiritual

---

[4] Those who are interested to learn more about the "confusion with dwelling in the womb" and the "splitting the yin" confusion, should consult more advanced books where these concepts will be explained.

cultivation constantly moves forward, never losing ground, never retreating.

There are four kinds of non-retreating:

1. In position, or in attainment: One will not fall back to the lesser position of ordinary people. This is from being able to bring along karma with rebirth to the Pure Land where ordinary people and sages cohabit.
2. In conduct: One will not regress in the Dharma practiced. One is reborn to the Pure Land where the Arhats and Pratyekabuddhas reside and one will never again regress to the state of confusion of ordinary people. Recall that Arhats and Pratyekabuddhas are sages at the Hinayana level.
3. In thoughts: There is no retreating in proper thoughts. One is reborn to the section of the Pure Land where the Bodhisattvas reside and will never regress to the states of the Arhats and Pratyekabuddhas, also known as the Two Vehicles.
4. Ultimate non-retreating: To hear the Buddha's name just once, whether with concentration or with a scattered mind, with belief or not, with understanding or not, creates the seeds for future liberation because it will be forever stored in our Alaya consciousness – the part of our mind that carries all our past karma, and that is reborn into a new body when we die. When all ignorance is ended, one can certify to ultimate non-retreating and will be reborn to the section of the Pure Land reserved for the Buddhas.

Attaining non-regression is one of the major advantages of getting to the Western Bliss Pure Land, since we will never again regress on our path to Buddhahood.

22. Invest In Your Future

Parents invest in the education of their children in order to give them a good life. Good companies make capital and human investments to increase their stockholders' wealth. Wise people invest in their retirement plan to provide security for themselves and their loved ones.

The bottom line is to set concrete goals and agree on specific timelines. It is important to invest in the near term as well as in the long-term.

This is important in the practice of Buddhism as well. Setting near term goals refers to this lifetime; setting long-term goals refers to future lifetimes.

For our purposes we will concentrate on spiritual goals, and leave other, non-spiritual goals to experts in their respective fields.

For this lifetime, we should strive to be as happy as possible. Happiness is a state of mind. Since most of us live in a community, our happiness depends in part on the happiness of others. For example, it is difficult to enjoy our own happiness when others around us are suffering.

Therefore, we can become happier if we can learn to make the others around us happier. This takes wisdom. Wisdom is fundamentally goodness to the core of our being.

In order to make our short stay on this earth more meaningful, we should invest our time and effort into learning how to treat our loved ones and family with more kindness and compassion, and then extend that compassion to our wider community, our country and the world.

If we learn to invest in improving our family, community and country so that those around us are better and happier, then we too will naturally become happier. Generous people experience more genuine happiness than those who are selfish, and have a more promising future.

Those who attempt to find happiness by over-indulging, and acquiring material wealth, will waste their blessings. Once their karmic bank account is empty, they will be prone to falling to the lower realms when they die. Further, the happiness that comes from accumulating wealth and power is ultimately unsatisfying. And those who self-indulge often do so at the expense of harming others, which only increases their chances of falling.

But those who are wise will plan for happiness in their future lives, as well as in this life. They know that the happiness that comes from helping others is much more genuine, and also generates good karma that will help them ascend after death.

Unfortunately, most worldly people are short-sighted and tend to neglect planning for future lives.

Wise people invest in creating blessings that will help them escape the Wheel of Birth and Death as soon as possible. They create the kinds of blessings that help them reach the Pure Land and progress with their cultivation of the

Dharma, rather than the kind of blessings that only help them reach the heavens.

The kind of blessings that arc best for this purpose are known as "blessings without outflows," which will be discussed in Chapter 35, "The Currency of Blessings."

I have a very smart disciple. She consistently understands most of the things I explain to her. So one day, I asked her about making investments. She responded, smart people should invest 75% into their current life and 25% into their next lives.

Do you agree with that?

Wise people invest increasingly more toward obtaining liberation, rather than becoming attached to this life, which is full of suffering and is temporary at best.

Moreover, those who manage to be reborn to the Pure Land experience only bliss. That is far more valuable than the immediate gratification and temporary happiness we experience in this life.

That is why one should not wait to make heavy investments into rebirth to the Western Bliss Pure Land.

For if not now, then when?

23. Faith: The First Requisite of Pure Land

The Pure Land practice is based on three key factors, known as the three requisites: Faith, Vows and Practice.

Faith is the foremost of the three requisites. Without faith, one cannot enter the Pure Land Dharma Door and make the vow to be reborn in Amitabha Buddha's Western Land. Similarly, without faith, one will not be motivated to practice this Dharma Door.

Buddhism teaches that faith – the belief in something you cannot see or prove – is the mother of all merit and virtue. Thus it is said that faith must come first. It is the beginning of cultivation.

Merit refers to what can be seen, such as being of direct service in helping others, for example, volunteering at a soup kitchen or other charitable work. Virtue refers to the inner goodness that is not visible or broadcasted, such as making private personal sacrifices in order to help others. Cultivating merit and virtue will help you increase your blessings.

There are several aspects to Faith. First, we should have faith in ourselves. We deserve to be reborn in the Pure Land. Even though we are not enlightened yet, we can carry our karma along to the Western Bliss Pure Land. Once we arrive there, our past karma cannot cause any more trouble and we can safely cultivate; this is unlike our Saha world where we are constantly faced with all sorts of obstructions and distractions.

In this world, those who resolve to cultivate commonly encounter numerous obstacles; for example, we might get a promotion at our job that requires us to work longer hours, allowing less time to cultivate at the temple on weekends.

At a deeper level, we must believe that we are endowed with the True Mind, which is not the mind with which we do mental processing, perform recognition and form perceptions. Our True Mind transcends time and space, and is beyond the reach of our intellect. Until we can see it for ourselves, we must have faith in it.

Just remember that all the worlds are simply manifestations of this True Mind, including the Western Bliss Pure Land. The Land of Utmost Bliss was purified by the mind of Bhikshu Dharma Treasury while he was on his causal grounds, cultivating the Bodhisattva path. Later Dharma Treasury Bhikshu became Amitabha Buddha, the leader of the Western Bliss Pure Land.

Next, we should have faith in others, as opposed to merely having faith in ourselves. The True Mind is present in everyone. However, we are still confused—that is why we don't know how to use our True Mind yet. Therefore, we should believe in the Buddha's True Mind. Living beings and the Buddhas all share the same nature. We are of the same substance. To believe in the Buddha is to believe in oneself.

We should trust that Shakyamuni and all the other Buddhas are speaking the truth when they praise the Pure Land

Dharma Door. They really are trying to help us quickly obtain liberation.

Next, believe in cause and effect. We already must have planted good roots in the past, in order to be encountering the Pure Land Dharma Door now. We should firmly believe that reciting the Buddha's name is the cause for rebirth. We ought to believe that rebirth of the multitude of sages in the Western Pure Land is powered by the three vows, and that we only have to follow them to make it to the secure place that is the Pure Land.

Rebirth to the Pure Land is the effect or fruition of practicing the Pure Land Dharma Door. We should deeply believe in the Western Bliss Pure Land. We can truly obtain rebirth there as a result of the Buddha Recitation Samadhi. As the patriarchs proclaimed: if we recite the Buddha's name, we will surely obtain rebirth to the Pure Land.

The Pure Land is no different from the pure mind. Since our mind is impure due to evil external influences, we can simply go to the Pure Land where we will be free from these external conditions that impede our progress. Then we will have a much easier time purifying our minds.

Next, believe in the noumena, or principles. We should believe that in principle, it is easier to obtain rebirth to the Pure Land through reliance on Amitabha Buddha's vow power.

We also should have faith in the phenomena, or manifestations. The Western Bliss Pure Land really exists just as all the Buddhas and Bodhisattvas say. Amitabha Buddha has great affinities with the living beings of our Saha world. He created his Pure Land Dharma Door in order to make it easier for us to get out of the revolving wheel of reincarnation.

Shakyamuni Buddha predicted that Pure Land Buddhism will be the Dharma Door of our era, and will help countless living beings. We can all believe in the Buddhas' words. According to *The Amitabha Sutra*, countless Buddhas of the ten directions praise Amitabha Buddha and urge us to seek rebirth to his country. Many great Bodhisattvas, amongst which the wisest of them all, Manjushri the Bodhisattva of Great Wisdom, also advocated rebirth to the Western Bliss Pure Land.

We would be well advised to follow in the footsteps of these great Bodhisattvas, and aim to reach Amitabha's Pure Land too.

24. Vows: The Second Requisite of Pure Land

Once we have faith, we should next make vows. Making vows is the second requisite of Pure Land practice.

Why? Because making vows will free us from the suffering of the Saha World and enable us to seek the peace and bliss of the Western Bliss Pure Land. Those who believe that they are well off and have no need for the Pure Land must realize that this short life is but a fleeting dream. The Saha world we live in is created by the defilements of our mind: that is why there is so much misery and suffering here. In contrast, the Pure Lands are created and adorned by the purification of our mind.

All Bodhisattvas in the past, present and future rely on Four Great Vows to realize Buddhahood. These Four Vows are:

1. I vow to save limitless living beings, according to the Truth of Suffering.
2. I vow to cut off the inexhaustible afflictions, according to the Truth of Origination.
3. I vow to study the immeasurable Dharma Doors, according to the Truth of the Way.
4. I vow to realize the supreme Buddha Way, according to the Truth of Extinction.

Making vows is important because it helps us align our

resources. When we sincerely make vows, seeds are planted and stored in our Alaya consciousness, where they serve as fuel to propel us toward rebirth to the Pure Lands. In particular, our vows create handles for the Buddhas and Bodhisattvas to come along and pull us to the Pure Lands.

The fact that we are still here, in this Saha World of suffering, means that we have failed in our prior cultivation and are still trapped in the reincarnation wheel. Our vows were not great enough, or sincere enough. Those who now wish to make vows for rebirth to the Pure Lands, must consider the following aspects:

We make vows to get out of the revolving wheel of reincarnation, permanently. Unless we can get out of this endless cycle of rebirth, we will continue to be born again and again, with very little control over where we go when we die and change bodies. If our good seeds mature, we will follow the good paths of the human and heavenly realms. However, if our bad seeds are activated, we will end up on the evil paths of the asura, animal, hungry ghost and hell realms. Those who understand the Dharma, will work toward escaping as soon as possible. We do not seek to enjoy worldly blessings in this lifetime, or in future lifetimes.

As we saw in Chapter 18, we make vows to horizontally escape the Triple Realm: the Desire Realm, Form Realm and Formless Realm. Do not seek to enjoy heavenly or earthly veneration and do not seek worldly karmic retributions like wealth and fame. (These are known as blessings with outflows, and will be further discussed in Chapter 35.)

Vow to universally save all living beings. Do not scheme to benefit only yourself, aspiring only for bliss and benefit in this one lifetime.

Vow to be reborn to the Pure Land as soon as possible. Do not be greedy for the Five Desires and joys of this turbid world, because they only make us stagnate and fail; they are empty and lack permanence.

Vow to realize your potential. Originally we were endowed with the True, efficacious Nature. Our confusion has allowed the afflictions of the world to obstruct and bind us. Now that we have obtained a human body, encountered the Buddhadharma, and heard of Amitabha Buddha's Dharma Door, we should be glad and resolve to draw near Amitabha Buddha, to hear the Dharma and to become enlightened to the Way.

We must not miss this opportunity. As the saying goes: "The Buddha is inside the mind, and yet people continue to seek outside. They are confused about the true, go chasing after the false, and thus miss the opportunity for one thousand autumns." If you can contemplate like this, then you can make a sincere vow on your own behalf to seek a place where you can live peacefully and safely.

Vow to end suffering and attain bliss. Suffering and bliss are direct opposites. In the Saha world, we are oppressed by a multitude of different types of suffering; in contrast, there is only bliss in the land of Utmost Bliss. In our world, the heavenly blessings are not permanent. The bliss in the Desire Heavens and first three Dhyana Heavens will eventually come to an end: that is the suffering of decay. When you are in samadhi of the Fourth Dhyana or in any of the four subsequent samadhi levels, you are free from coarse suffering and bliss but still experience subtle forms of suffering, called the activity skandha; please refer to more advanced books on Buddhism for this concept.

As a result, when your heavenly blessings are exhausted, you will fall. As Dharma Master YongJia says in his *Song of Enlightenment*: "Practicing giving and observing precepts will produce heavenly blessings; it's like shooting an arrow into the sky; when the force is exhausted the arrow will fall, bringing undesirable consequences in future lives."

The following story will further illustrate this point.

Once, there was a Taoist named Lu Chun Yang who paid a visit to Chan Master Yellow Dragon. Lu first hid under the bell tower to listen to the master's sutra lecture. Master Yellow Dragon knew, and declared that there was a Dharma thief in the assembly. Lu heard the Master, and immediately came out, saying: "I already have the immortality dharma. Why would I need to steal your Dharma?" The Chan Master simply replied, "You are a corpse guardian ghost." Lu was unimpressed and asked, "One grain contains the entire world, a half-liter pot can cook the three thousand worlds: what is that state?" The Chan master replied, "Even if you can live for 80,000 kalpas, it's just like dying in empty space." Lu had an immediate awakening. He abandoned Taoism and became Buddhist. The immortals failed to understand that long life or life in the heavens was not free from suffering. Through the Pure Land Dharma Door, however, we can escape and end birth and death.

Vow not to regress. The Western Bliss Pure Land residents are all avaivartikas: they have attained the state of "non-regression." In contrast, in this Saha world, living beings commit heavy offenses and therefore encounter severe obstructions. Cultivating here is like rowing a boat upstream: it is hard to make headway and easy to fall back. This is because most people lack a solid and strong vow to sustain their faith and practice. As we have seen, out of a million people, it is difficult for even one individual to succeed in cultivation. Either they quit early because they lack determination, or eventually quit down the line because they encounter demonic obstructions, or evil friends.

Typically, their life comes to an end before they have accomplished anything of importance. Once born into a new body, they forget everything, and must start over again. It's not easy to succeed in this turbid world unless you have deep roots and have proper knowledge. Even in this case, if the conditions are unfavorable, then prior cultivation may be lost; if the conditions are favorable, we may still face obstructions because we tend to chase after material things.

Even the Tenth Faith Bodhisattvas[5], who have already brought forth the great resolve to cultivate, will sometimes progress and sometimes regress. Like a feather floating in space, Bodhisattvas who cultivate the Ten Faiths must pass through 10,000 kalpas (there are around 16 million years in one kalpa) for the mind of faith to be complete, their good roots to mature and for them to certify to the First

---

[5] The Ten Faiths are among the stages of practice through which Bodhisattvas must progress on their path to Buddhahood.

Dwelling[6]. At this point they can be assured that they will no longer regress.

As stated in Chapter 21 on Irreversibility, the technical Buddhist term for this stage is non-regression in position. If you recite the Buddha's name and obtain rebirth to the Western Bliss Pure Land, you can immediately certify to the three non-regressions in position, practice and mind.

Vow to be born by transformation on a lotus flower and personally see Amitabha Buddha. Then this life will not have been in vain. *The Dharma Flower Sutra* (also known as *The Lotus Sutra*) says: "For a Buddha to appear in the world is rare like the utpala flower." We are born in the Dharma ending age, after the Buddha entered Nirvana. Yet we are blessed enough to obtain this human body and have the opportunity to practice the Pure Land Dharma. Therefore, we should seize the opportunity and make the resolve for Bodhi, vow to be born on a golden lotus dais and personally see Amitabha Buddha.

---

[6] After passing through the Ten Faiths, Bodhisattvas must next accomplish the Ten Dwellings, which are further stages of a Bodhisattva's practice.

25. Practice: The Third Requisite of Pure Land

The third and final requisite of the Pure Land Dharma Door is practice. We must take action in order to attain our goal.

Inadequate vow power will not lead to practice. Practice is like tossing the water-clearing pearl into the mud, magically clearing the muddy water. When the Buddha's name enters a confused mind, the confused mind becomes a Buddha mind. Practice can increase sincerity.

However, those who practice the recitation Dharma Door but have not yet purified their minds encounter many kinds of obstructions such as: inadequate faith, insincere vows, an afflicted mind, attachment to worldly affairs, etc. If you wish to overcome your obstructions, you must use the proper methods and, ideally, have proper guidance from a wise teacher. If you can find these, and if you are persistent and do not quit, then eventually you will succeed in your practice.

The most common form of practice is often referred to as "reciting the Buddha's name."

As was explained in the "Only Ten Recitations" Chapter, we ultimately practice reciting the Buddha's name in order to attain the state of having "one mind unconfused," also known as the Buddha Recitation Samadhi, so that we can be assured of rebirth at the end of this lifetime.

However, the Pure Land practice is not confined to the method of reciting the Buddha's name. The Pure Land Dharma Door also includes other important Buddhist practices, such as the Six Paramitas and the Ten Thousand Practices. In fact, all other forms of Mahayana cultivation are part of Pure Land practice as well. For instance, all of the following practices can aid in obtaining rebirth to the Pure Land:

- Making offerings

  Making offerings to the Triple Jewel is a good way to build up your blessings.
- Transferring Merit

  After doing something good, you can give away the good karma you have generated, and dedicate it to all beings, wishing that they be reborn to Amitabha's Land of Ultimate Bliss.
- Repentance Dharmas

  If we fail to repent, the bad karma from offenses we have been creating since beginningless time will eventually overwhelm us. Chapter 40 of the Avatamsaka Sutra describes repentance Dharmas in detail.
- Bowing

  Both a physical and a spiritual exercise, bowing is a form of repentance Dharma and can also help to reduce the ego.
- Observing precepts

If you follow the precepts and do not harm others, you will receive protection and others will not harm you.

- Reciting Sutras

  The Amitabha Sutra is commonly recited among Purc Land practitioners, but actually reciting any Mahayana Sutra is part of the Pure Land Dharma Door as well.
- Maintaining Mantras

  The Rebirth Mantra is most commonly used in Pure Land practice, but, as with Sutras, all Mahayana mantras are also included in the Pure Land Dharma Door.

We will explain how to cultivate some of these additional practices in Part VI. However, to describe all of these practices in detail are beyond the scope of this book; they are only mentioned to make you aware of the many other Dharmas that are included in Mahayana.

For now, the important point to remember is that we need not limit ourselves to reciting the Buddha's name, to the exclusion of all other Dharma Doors.

This is not to say that one must perfect all of these practices to be reborn. However, if one wishes to make it to the Pure Land, having some form of practice is of critical importance.

Finally, we will discuss some of the more advanced states of recitation. These states may be inaccessible to most readers; in that case, don't think too much about them. Instead just read with an open mind and you will be planting seeds that will germinate in the future.

Reciting the Buddha's name can be classified into two categories: phenomenon and noumenon recitation. Phenomenon means "manifestation," and refers to the changing world of events that we experience moment by moment. Noumenon, on the other hand, means "principles." In particular, noumenon refers to the unchanging true principles of the Dharma.

Phenomenon 事持 recitation refers to the act of bringing forth deep faith without skepticism after hearing of the Pure Land Dharma. One thus recites single-mindedly and clearly, in thought after thought, whether sitting, standing, lying down or walking. No other thought exists but the Buddha's name. If one can maintain the Buddha's name this way, one can free oneself of all afflictions. However, in phenomenon recitation, one has not yet penetrated the noumenon.

In practicing Phenomenon recitation, we use the mind, the subject, to recite the Buddha's name, the object. Subject and object are clear and distinct. When the mind and Buddha, subject and object, are in accord, then mind is not apart from Buddha and Buddha is not apart from the mind. One is clearly aware of the uninterrupted recitation. The concentrated mind dispels the false, as the frozen lake stops the flow of water. Then the Buddha is like the autumn moon shining in space—clear, brilliant and unmoving. We can thus enter samadhi. This state is described in the Han Shan poem:

My mind is like the autumn moon,
Or a green pool that is pure and clear.
Nothing can compare.
How can I express it!

After attaining phenomenon recitation, one can go on to attain noumenon recitation.

As in phenomenon recitation, in noumenon recitation 理持 one first recites to the utmost until one enters emptiness. One then is able to understand that outside of the mind that recites, there is no Buddha. And outside of the Buddha, there is no mind that can recite. Mind and Buddha are one and the same, one same substance. Both subject and object disappear, and the marks of the self and Buddha merge. One recites and yet does not recite. Conversely, one does not recite and yet recites, thus penetrating the principles.

At this stage, one is no longer confused by the two extremes of existence and emptiness. In noumenon recitation, the mind that recites the Buddha's name neither dwells in existence or falls into emptiness. It dwells and yet does not dwell; it dwells in the Middle Way of the principle nature. One can then continue to recite until one sees one's own Buddha nature.

The ancients say:

> *Suddenly the thought of Amitabha arises*;
> *The ground is leveled, there is no wind, a wave arises by itself*;
> *Thought after thought dissipates and returns to non-thought thought*;
> *Even knowing of non-thought is excessive*!

When you reach this state, there is a block of empty spiritual essence, and the principle nature reveals itself.

The principle nature is also known as Real Mark. Real Mark is the absence of marks. It is non-dual: not inside or outside or in between; not in the past, present or future; not black or white, long or short, square or circular, having no odor or touch or taste. Look for it and it cannot be found. Speak of it and it cannot be expressed. It can create the thousand worlds and you cannot fathom its limits. It is apart from all conditions and discernment, separate from words and language and yet words and language are not different from it. It is still and yet can move. Stillness and movement are not dual. Body and Pure Land are not dual.

There is no mark: this is referred to as True Emptiness. And yet there is nothing that is not marked: this is referred to as Wonderful Existence. Other names for Real Mark are True Suchness, the one True Dharma Realm, the Thus Come One's Store Nature.

These descriptions of more advanced states of Pure Land practice are drawn from our commentary on *The Small Amitabha Sutra*[7], which the reader may wish to consult for more detail. Additional information on these kinds of states can also be found in *The Three Essentials of Pure Land*, a collection of Dharma talks by Luò Jì Hé 駱季和.

One should not try to understand these types of descriptions with one's rational mind. These states are only mentioned to plant seeds in one's mind, which one will eventually come to understand through one's own experience, rather than through reading or intellectual study.

It may be awhile before you reach these levels of recitation, but don't worry about it; your practice will unfold in time. Being greedy to attain these states will only hinder your progress.

---

[7] The Small Amitabha Sutra with commentary is available at www.chanpureland.org/publications.

For now, focus on learning the basics. Part VI of this book will give you some concrete tools that you can practice. The harder you work at these, the more you will understand.

Practice requires genuine effort; and the kind of effort that is required can only follow deep faith and sincere vows.

Again, Faith, Vows, and Practice: these are the three requisites for the Pure Land Dharma Door. They are like a three-legged bronze incense urn that needs each leg to stand and function. Those who take rebirth seriously should cultivate all three, since they are all integral to the practice.

26. Renaissance of Pure Land Buddhism

We are currently in a unique position to revive and strengthen Buddhism for the benefit of ourselves and future generations. And the Pure Land Dharma can play a significant role in this endeavor.

In the United States, Mahayana Buddhism has just begun to take root and the Proper Dharma does not yet have a firm foundation. And in most Buddhist countries in Asia, modernization and the drive to adopt Western values has dramatically weakened the Dharma, and begun to distort Buddha's teachings and deviate from the proper principles.

Our current Dharma Ending Era might, in regard to Buddhism, be compared to the Dark Ages that occurred in Europe from the 5th to 15th Centuries.

Fortunately, as the Great Master Xuan Hua taught us, those who practice the Proper Dharma, remain in the Proper Dharma Era, even as the world around them may be in the Dharma Ending Era. If we can inspire people to live according to the Buddha's teachings, then we can mitigate the destructive potential of our current period. The more people who lead lives of goodness and virtue, the more that the areas where they live will become prosperous and be free of calamities and natural disasters.

Thanks to its ability to benefit people of all different capacities, from "superior" to "inferior" roots, the Pure

Land Dharma will be critical to this process. Thus we would be wise to look at the history of Pure Land Buddhism in China.

Chinese culture is very profound, in part because it was heavily influence by Buddhism for thousands of years. For instance, Buddhist principles permeate the idioms and stories that are woven into the fabric of Chinese language and culture.

As the most widespread form of Buddhism in China, the Pure Land School was critical in this integration of Buddhist values into everyday Chinese culture.

Today, China is known as a manufacturing and exporting powerhouse, supplying goods around the world. Less known, but far more significant, is that the Chinese popularized and exported Pure Land Buddhism throughout Asia, where it continues to be widely practiced.

Shakyamuni Buddha taught the Pure Land Dharma during his lifetime. When he was teaching in India, he spoke the Amitabha Sutra, which was recorded as part of the original Sanskrit cannon. However, the Pure Land methods were not widely practiced until they reached China, where the Great Master Huì Yuǎn 慧遠 (AD 334-416) of the Jìn 晉 dynasty officially founded the Chinese Pure Land School.

As we consider how to best integrate the Pure Land methods in our current context, it may help to look at the example set by Master Huì Yuǎn. He came from a very modest family background. As he was very diligent in his studies, Master Huì Yuǎn was erudite and specialized in the Confucian classic texts. One day, he was listening to Great Master Dào An 道安 lecture on the Prajna Sutra, and he was suddenly awakened. He immediately left the home-life.

His awe-inspiring comportment would often render those who met with him speechless and flustered. Soon his "Way virtue," his virtuous conduct as a monk, was well known throughout the land.

In AD 382, Master Huì Yuǎn traveled to Lu Mountain 廬山 and saw ample land that belonged to no one. He took a rest. That night a mountain spirit appeared in his dream, while at the same time it began thundering and raining in torrents. This was unusual because there was a severe drought in the area. In addition, normally the ground was parched and dry. But when Master Huì Yuǎn tapped his cane on the ground, water would flow out. Later, Master Huì Yuǎn set up a platform by a pond and recited the Sea Dragon King Sutra 海龍王經. A giant dragon arose from the pond and it rained heavily again. These and other manifestations persuaded Master Huì Yuǎn to stay at Lu Mountain and cultivate.

The prefecture governor heard of these responses, and came to believe in Master Huì Yuǎn. Eventually, the governor even built a Buddha Hall, which he named Heavenly Sent, in which Master Huì Yuǎn could cultivate and teach others.

Master Huì Yuǎn aspired for rebirth to the Western Bliss Pure Land. He built lotus-shaped sun-dials and recited the Buddha's name without interruption. In time, Master Huì Yuǎn founded a group of cultivators known as the Lotus Society. Together, they lived and cultivated on Lu Mountain, and specialized in reciting the Buddha's name. Many high level monastics, officials and famous scholars came to Lu Mountain to practice with the Master. In all, there were 140 people who were devoted to Pure Land practice.

Master Huì Yuǎn taught on the Lu Mountain for 30 years and never left the area. Even when he escorted guests who were returning to their homes, he never left the mountain.

All the members of the Lotus Society obtained numerous responses. The term "response," here, refers to the fact that their prayers were answered, fulfilling their wishes. For example, Great Master Huì Yuǎn himself once saw Amitabha Buddha flanked by the two Great Bodhisattvas, Guan Yin and Great Strength, and accompanied by a Great Assembly. Their bodies filled empty space. He saw wondrous light flowing back and forth in 14 streams. He experienced the light to be speaking the Dharma. Amitabha Buddha then certified to the Master that, because of his past vows, he would be reborn in the Western Bliss Pure Land. Amongst the assembly that appeared in his vision, the Master also saw past members of the Lotus Society who already had made it to the Pure Land.

The Great Master was ecstatic! He told his followers of the news and informed them that he saw Amitabha Buddha, along with Guan Yin and Great Strength Bodhisattvas. In fact, he told his followers that he had seen the Three Sages of the West on three previous occasions. This was the fourth time they had appeared to him.

As predicted by Amitabha Buddha, the Great Master passed away shortly afterward, while sitting in meditation in AD 417. He was 83 years old. Great Master Huì Yuǎn was named first patriarch of the Pure Land sect.

It is said that all the practitioners of his Lotus Society went to the Western Bliss Pure Land.

Because of its broad appeal and many benefits, today Pure Land Buddhism remains the most popular form of Buddhist practice in many parts of Asia, especially in China, Japan, and Korea. This popularity can partly be explained by the written records of the numerous responses experienced by its practitioners. These records document stories of people who have died and made it to Pure Land, as revealed through various signs. Just as in other religions, people have faith because they, or the people they know, have obtained such responses. Today, many Pure Land Practitioners continue to achieve rebirth to the Western Bliss Pure Land, perhaps because Amitabha Buddha still has not given up on us confused people yet.

If this wonderful Chinese export becomes better understood, then more living beings will be able to benefit from this Dharma Door. In many instances today, faith in Pure Land Buddhism relies more on tradition and culture than on clear knowledge. Buddhism, however, is about wisdom, not blind faith or superstition. While many Buddhist believers still put their faith in Pure Land Buddhism, many monastics no longer have a good understanding of its principles and practice. In order to understand the Pure Land Dharma Door, practitioners must all vigorously work on, and strengthen their recitation samadhi (their concentration level).

Monastics, or "left-home people," should make it their responsibility to perfect their recitation practice and strengthen their samadhi so they can develop the skills to build Buddhist cultivation centers to train the next generation. Such cultivation centers will also make the principles of the Proper Dharma accessible to all those who wish to learn.

Following in the footsteps of Great Master Huì Yuǎn, we should also establish communities of practitioners, like

Master Huì Yuǎn's Lotus Societies, dedicated to helping send people to the Western Bliss Pure Land.

If we can succeed in these aspirations, then we will truly be on our way toward creating a renaissance of Pure Land Buddhism.

IV

Pure Lands, Heavens, and Hells

27. Pure Land Buddhism and Other Religions

Belief in the heavens and hells is a common thread found in many religious traditions, so this section will also provide an opportunity for some comparative points on Buddhism and other religions.

Different cultures in this world have many wonderful religious practices and beliefs that are of great value. If more people truly lived according to the teachings of these religions, this world would be far better off.

Since Christianity plays such a central role in Western culture, this chapter will draw some general comparisons with Pure Land Buddhism. Some of the points considered here may also apply with respect to other religions as well; Christianity is mentioned only by way of example, and since it has been so central to the Western culture that is now influencing the entire world.

However, this is not the place for detailed comparisons between Christianity and Buddhism. Such a discussion is too complex for this book, and is of questionable value to the practice of either religion.

Further, comparisons will not be drawn between the Christian heaven and the Pure Land. Even within Christianity, there is no single accepted concept of heaven.

The Buddhist texts give more specific descriptions of the heavens than Christianity does (see the next chapter), but we will leave it to the reader to draw parallels between these descriptions and their own personal understanding of heaven. Both Christianity and Buddhism recognize that most of us do not have the capacity to truly resolve the problems of the human condition. In Buddhism, the central problem is spelled out in terms of suffering, whereas the Christian teachings are phrased more in terms of sin. Yet the obvious shared principle is that we must cultivate goodness if we wish to improve.

Buddhism outlines a detailed path of practice whereby we can overcome suffering and see our True Nature. However, this path is admittedly so difficult that very few can walk on it, and no one can complete it in a single lifetime. Therefore, like Christianity, Pure Land Buddhism teaches us the advantages of finding some help along the way.

Those who have faith in the Christian God and Jesus Christ, can find what Christians define as salvation. Along their path, they may request help from Jesus, God and the saints through prayer. Likewise, those who have affinities with Buddhism, can receive help in their cultivation from Amitabha Buddha.

In the Pure Land teachings, this kind of help is known as "other's power," and is contrasted with "self power."

Our cultivation is like rowing a boat: we can make faster progress when we not only use our own effort to row, but we also set our sails to harness the power of the wind. In the Pure Land Dharma Door, self and other's power work together as we cross the vast ocean of suffering to reach the other shore of Nirvana.

Anyone who would like to study Buddhist principles and techniques is welcome to do so, regardless of their religious background. People from other faiths are welcome to learn from Buddhist principles, and even those who may be skeptical of all faith-based traditions, often study Buddhism to learn practical techniques to develop their concentration power and live happier lives.

It should already be clear that this book is presented from the Mahayana Buddhist perspective. It is by no means an unbiased account, but will outline the advantages of Buddhism, so that the reader can best make up her own mind what practices are best for her.

That said, according to Buddhism, all the heavens, of any religion, share the same fundamental difference with the Pure Lands: namely, the heavens do not lead to a permanent escape from the wheel of reincarnation. However, this is precisely what the Pure Lands are designed to help us do.

Thus, for those who wish to end their suffering and pursue enlightenment, the Pure Lands are the best places to go.

Also, recall that those who reach the Pure Land are free to travel all over the Dharma Realm. By riding on Amitabha's spiritual powers, they may come and go as they please. In fact, this is one of the better aspects of the Pure Land: if you make it there, you can look around and experience things for yourself. Because Amitabha shares his spiritual powers with everyone in the Pure Land, you can instantly travel anywhere in the cosmos. And if you don't like it in the Pure Land, you can leave any time. There is no better money back guarantee!

This is important Buddhist wisdom that we wish to share, but it is not intended to deter those who aspire to reach the heavens. Anyone who practices goodness is moving in the right direction.

Know that the Buddhas and Bodhisattvas wish to save all living beings and do not discriminate between Christians, Muslims, Buddhists, etc.

These are merely human labels.

The Buddhas and Bodhisattvas will do their best to help everyone.

28. The Heavens vs. The Pure Lands

According to the law of karma, if we do good things, then we will reap good results. Just as pleasure and happiness are earned in this world, pleasure and happiness may be earned at a higher level in the heavens and the Pure Lands.

While both those who reach the heavens and those who make it to the Pure Lands will experience very blissful states, the heavenly rewards are not permanent. Bound to time, they eventually run out, returning one to the continuous cycle of life in other realms. Only in Pure Land will one attain a permanent end to the cycle of reincarnation – a place to cultivate in peace, enjoying one's blessings, paradoxically, without the attachment to desire; a place to enjoy the rewards of our good karma, while escaping the inevitable decay of those very rewards.

Although the inhabitants of the Pure Land also have limited lifespans, they can be assured that they will attain true permanence by becoming Buddhas, before the end of their life. Those who are born to the heavens, on the other hand, are still far from true permanence.

According to Buddhism, the Buddha was able to see the structure of the entire cosmos, including all of the heavens. Others who have opened their Spiritual Eye, though their vision is not as complete as the Buddha's, will also be able to confirm many of the following descriptions of the heavens.

Each galaxy, known in Buddhism as a "Buddhaland" or simply a "world," consists of the following Three Realms:

1. The Desire Realm
2. The Form Realm
3. The Formless Realm

Our Saha World, known to scientists as the Milky Way galaxy, shares this same structure.

According to the Buddha's teachings, the everyday world in which we live, the world of humans, is located in the Desire Realm. Above our human world are six heavens that exist in the Desire Realm with our human world; the remaining heavens are located in the Form and Formless Realms. The Form and Formless Realms consist entirely of heavens.

As the name suggests, the inhabitants of the Desire Realm like to indulge in their desires. In general, there are five kinds of desires of the senses. Namely, the desires for:

1. Sex: This is the most powerful driving force in humanity. We are prepared to move mountains and dry up oceans to satisfy this desire.
2. Food: While we take pleasure in eating, according to Buddhism, eating is actually a form of illness.

Food is considered medicine for our body. It's very good medicine[8].

3. Sleep: Our body needs to shut down for repairs periodically, especially after exertions such as sex or over-eating.
4. Fame: Our ego continually demands recognition and praise.
5. Wealth: We crave the sense of security, power and achievement that wealth brings.

The vast majority of human endeavors are for the sake of satisfying desires by chasing after externals. When our desires are fulfilled, we temporarily feel happy. When they are not, we are miserable. As a result, our existence is filled with anxiety.

The sutras describe that the Six Desire Heavens of the Desire Realm are located above our human world. The beings who live in these heavens, as well as in the heavens located in the Form and Formless Realms, are all referred to as gods in Buddhism.

The gods in the Desire Realm still have desires for food, sex and sleep. They have marriages as in the human realm,

---

[8] To some, this may be an unfamiliar way of looking at food, but think about it like this: Our bodies are constantly deteriorating, and without fuel to make ongoing repairs, we would be unable to function. We are so used to this dependency that we regard it as natural, but actually it is a kind of sickness that we all must undergo.

only the heavenly pleasures are far greater than those in the human realm.

Above the Desire Realm is the Form Realm. All the gods who reside there have samadhi power and are consequently free from desires for sex, sleep and food. However, they have not uprooted those desires. Rather, these kinds of desire have simply become latent. Gods of The Form Realm are very attached to their form body, which is very refined.

The gods of the Formless Realm, however, are free from the attachment to their form body. For example, the various Hindu gods such Vishnu and Shiva exist in the Formless Realm.

Gods are born to enjoy their heavenly blessings. It is a far more wonderful existence than our human condition. The higher the Realm, the more bliss one can experience. The resultant bliss far surpasses the pleasure from the senses that we can have here in the Desire Realm. Meditation practitioners, and those who have opened their spiritual eye, can also experience these realms.

While humans have to earn a living, the gods in the Desire Realm do not have to go to work at all. They live in palaces with their families.

The bodies of the gods in all of the Desire Realms are free from disease. In fact, they do not ever have to bathe or wash their clothes.

How is such an existence possible? This question can be turned around: why is such an existence believed to be impossible?

People who manage to work hard and save money can start living like a king in our human realm. The principle involved here is the same: if you save enough, then such a lifestyle will be affordable. It's all about cause and effect. For instance, the Christian practice of charity is one of the major reasons why many Christians will be able go to the Desire heavens to be nearer to their God. They are very wise and know that if they plant the right causes, they will achieve the desired effect.

However, just like anything else, such an existence does not last forever. Remember, according to the law of cause and effect, all good lives are the result of blessings created in the past. When one's blessings are used up, one becomes poorer. Eventually, the gods too, must return to the reincarnation wheel and change into another body and another realm of existence. As mentioned in the previous chapter, Buddhism teaches that this is true of all the heavens, from any religion.

Of course Buddhists do not mind going to the heavens and enjoying the good life. However, the wise Buddhist prefers to go to the Pure Lands.

The advantage of the Pure Lands over the heavens is that heavenly beings are attached to pleasures or bliss and are not free of suffering, whereas those in the Pure Lands, as we have seen, will cultivate until they end all suffering and attain Buddhahood.

For example, all the wonders that the gods enjoy while in the Desire Heavens will eventually decay. Though they have a very long lifespan, in time, even the gods will have to die. When they are about to die, they begin to perspire and smell bad for the first time in their lives. After a lifetime of incredible bliss, the fact that they still have to suffer in the end makes them miserable.

Inhabitants of the Pure Land enjoy similar heavenly blessings. They do not have to work. They eat heavenly food, swim in heavenly pools, and live in heavenly palaces. In fact, everything in the Pure Lands is even more refined than in the heavens.

Different levels of social status exist in the Pure Land too. For example, in the Western Bliss Pure Land, there are nine different grades of rebirth. Those with more blessings are born into higher grades and experience greater bliss. For more detail, one can consult the Pure Land scriptures.

Inhabitants of the Pure Land choose cultivation over confusion and over the futile search for external pleasure and gratification. As a result, they are all happier.

As we mentioned earlier, pleasure and happiness are earned. That is why the Buddhist scriptures refer to those who are reborn to the Pure Lands as "good men and women with superior causes and conditions." They have accrued many more blessings than it takes to go to the heavens.

Of course, many people in this world have affinities with Christianity or other religions, and their goal is to reach heaven. But the Mahayana Buddhist perspective shows the lack of permanence of such a choice – and it is a choice: Do you wish to permanently stop cycling through the wheel of reincarnation?

If the answer is "Yes," then working toward rebirth into the Pure Lands, in this lifetime, should be the goal.

Very few people have the privilege and blessings to hear about the Pure Land, let alone to be reborn there. Those who know about it, need not settle for anything less.

29. The Hells Await the Hateful

Many people don't believe in the hells. Here we will not attempt to argue with them or prove that the hells exist. Instead we will explore some of the different facets of this important Buddhist teaching, and share some of the descriptions of the hells that have been handed down to us, through the Buddhist scriptures, by those wiser than ourselves.

The hells exist in both mental and physical states.

First of all, the hells are a state of mind. When we experience mental torture, whether due to abuse by others, or our own internal states, as in depression, we may feel so much suffering that we want to die. It is no surprise that many people take their own lives in order to end this kind of intense pain.

Such thoughts of suicide, no matter how short-lived, may have crossed many of our minds. When distress is unbearable, one naturally wants it to end. Many of us go through these extreme emotions at least once in our lives, to the point that we would consider this radical solution of self-destruction.

Since most of us understand what mental torment entails, we should strive not to inflict the same suffering on others through unloving actions, dishonesty, cruelty, or other selfishness.

In addition to mental anguish, we may experience physical hell on earth; we may endure warfare, extreme poverty, chronic physical pain, severe illness, crime, bad marriages and other unhealthy relationships, and so on.

Living in prison can be likened to hell because there may be a lack of light, basic material comforts, safety and personal rights. A highly compensated engineer, who had been sent to a jail where hardened criminals were housed, later reported that he was "conditioned" with the severe cold of the jail cells and the constant threat of being abused by his fellow prisoners. Previously, he used to walk around with his head held high; now he would walk with his eyes lowered so as to avoid looking at other prisoners.

Clearly, there is hell on earth. It should be no surprise that the hells also exist as a separate plane of being. According to Buddhism, the hells are physically located beneath the earth.

The hells are well documented in the Earth Store Sutra. Basically, the hells are reserved for those who must undergo severe torture for their heavy offenses. They must go through extreme suffering for having inflicted extreme suffering on others. Such is the law of cause and effect. Enduring the suffering is one way to eradicate past evil deeds.

We will now share some of the descriptions of the hells given in the Buddhist sutras. This detail is included to set a stark contrast with the Pure Land, where the three lower paths of the animal, ghost and hell realms do not even exist.

Why is this? Because in the Pure Land, no one creates any offenses; therefore the hells do not arise. This is a tremendous advantage over our Saha world, where it is so easy to create offenses for which we may subsequently spend eons undergoing heavy retributions.

The hells are dark: not a single glimmer of sunlight or moonlight breaks through the gloom. To exit these terrible places, offenders must rely on their blessings. Hopefully, their family and friends are aware of their hardship, and will make offerings to generate blessings on their behalf. Otherwise, they will remain in a state of torment until retribution is completed.

In the human realm, torture is generally forbidden, even in the "hell-on-earth places" such as prisons or concentration camps; yet being tortured is a way of life in the hells below, where the prisoners are routinely tortured to death. But as soon as they die, a "clever breeze" blows and resuscitates the prisoners, so that they can undergo torture over and over again. In the hells, each day may involve tens of thousands of deaths.

The Buddha taught that there are different hells with punishments corresponding to the varying degrees of offenses one has committed. The worst hell of them all is called Avici, Sanskrit for relentless or unending. In this hell, there is absolutely no break in the suffering and torture for millions of years of each lifespan. The prisoners typically must go through millions of such lifespans in this type of hell where there is virtually no hope for escape until their term is up.

Those who abused their power to harm others will face the four gates of the Squeezing Mountains hell. The mountains in this hell open to let the denizens escape. However, as they are about to escape, two of the mountains will swiftly move together and crush them to death.

Precept-holders who broke their precepts will experience the retribution of falling into the Iron Clothing hell, where knives with hooks will rip their clothes apart. As the naked prisoners wish for clothing, a set of metallic clothes will drop out of the sky and garb them. However, the clothing is made of hot iron, and will burn the precept-breakers to ashes. Subsequently, a "clever wind" will blow through the area to resurrect the dead, and the torture will be repeated.

Precept-holders who broke the third precept of infidelity and those who had sexual relationships outside marriage, are said to fall into the Embracing Pillar hell. There, the offender will mistake a hot copper pillar as his or her beloved one, and hug it. The hot copper pillar will burn him or her to death. Again, a "clever wind" will then come to cool off the area and bring the dead person back to life, and the hugging and burning process will be repeated. This is the hell for people with the karma of lust.

People who slandered and wrecked the Triple Jewel will be subjected to the Plowing Tongues hell. There, evil ghosts will lift the prisoners into the air by hooks imbedded in the prisoner's tongues. This is the retribution for having influenced others not to believe in the Buddha through slander and lies. In addition, people who engaged in "mouth karmas" will also pave their way to the Plowing Tongues hell. The four types of mouth karma are: 1) harsh speech, 2) divisive speech, 3) frivolous speech, and 4) false speech.

People who committed killing offenses, having killed living beings such as bugs, birds, or animals, will eventually end up in the Hacking Heads hell.

According to the Buddha's teachings, there are countless types of hells, each containing all sorts of torture instruments to make sure that we undergo the proper retribution for our past offenses.

The sure fire way to go to the hells is to indulge in anger or hatred. Because of anger, we are prepared to make life "like hell" for our victims. That is why we eventually must go to one or more of the hells to pay back our debts.

Even those who do not believe in the hells may nonetheless fall there after they die. Fortunately, they can still receive help from their loved ones, thanks to special Dharmas that are available to Buddhists; but it is better to take precautionary measures to ensure that this doesn't happen.

V

At the Time of Death

30. Self Help Versus Other's Help

Previously, in the "Only Ten Recitations" chapter, we explained that assured of rebirth to the Western Bliss Pure Land if we manage to recite the Buddha's name 10 times with one mind unconfused. This is primarily self-help, because we must rely on our own recitation samadhi to succeed.

The purpose of our Buddha recitation training program is to teach you how to enter this samadhi. The goal is to build your recitation samadhi so that you can help yourself and not be a burden on others. However, we have already mentioned that it is not easy to achieve the Buddha Recitation Samadhi; in fact, most of us will not do so in one lifetime.

This is where one of the major advantages of Pure Land Buddhism becomes relevant: practitioners can get help from others in gaining rebirth to the Pure Land.

How can others help? They can help in two ways.

First, others can recite on our behalf. If they can enter the Buddha Recitation Samadhi themselves, then they can certainly notify Amitabha Buddha and bring our name to his awareness. This will only help if they are credible enough with Amitabha for him to honor their request. Second, others can also give us their rebirth blessings, thus enabling us to earn our place in the Pure Land.

The Buddhist tradition of enlisting the help of left-home people to help the deceased draws on both of these concepts. During the 49-day period after the death of a friend or relative, people will often request monastics to recite and perform ceremonies on behalf of the deceased. These ceremonies are designed to transfer rebirth blessings into their karmic bank account.

This is a very valuable tradition that is worth maintaining. Unfortunately, however, rebirth to the Pure Land seems to have become *merely* a tradition or custom instead of a major undertaking, as it should be. The substance behind the tradition is usually lacking.

Consequently, most Pure Land adherents are reduced to requesting the temple's help more out of cultural custom than out of true understanding. While this is certainly better than the custom of partying and drinking to commemorate the deceased, it still falls far short of what needs to be done to aid in getting rebirth to the Pure Land.

It doesn't help that funerals are so expensive. Worse yet, the majority of funerals are of little help to the deceased. Consequently, most of the dead do not make it to the Pure Land.

Funerals may provide a rite of passage and a way of dealing with the grief on the part of those left behind. However, those whose resources are limited, and who believe in the Pure Land Dharma, may wish to avoid spending a fortune on ceremonial and ornamental things that are primarily for appearances, and instead judiciously use their resources to help the deceased.

If you truly wish to help your deceased loved ones, you must be very sincere and you must seek the right kind of help. Obtaining other's help for rebirth hinges on:

1. The other's recitation ability, and/or
2. Their rebirth blessings.

Whereas many people typically consult more than one doctor before major surgeries, most Buddhists would simply walk into the nearest temple to request help on behalf of the deceased in an effort to save their loved ones from the grips of their mortal enemies.

The wise ones, however, would conduct a more thorough search. They would talk to at least a few temples to see what they propose, and would then choose the one that is better qualified in the two qualifications mentioned above.

Those who are truly blessed will do their own research and prepare ahead of time. Should you feel that you cannot manage to get to the Pure Land through your own recitation strength, then you may wish to arrange ahead of time to have qualified help for when you die.

31. Forty-Nine Days To Go

Death is a subject that few of us like to discuss. As medical technology improves, the subject of death becomes more removed from our daily awareness. With good and improving healthcare, we hope, and seem, to cheat death for decades longer than history has allowed.

As a result, fear of death, and a desire to remove it from our consciousness, has been more prevalent in the last 100 years or so.

In this chapter, we will discuss death – how Buddhists prepare for its inevitability, and what to expect in the critical 49-day period after death.

The information presented here is based on the Buddhist Sutras, such as *The Earth Store Sutra.* Readers can consult the Buddhist texts for more details.

We have already mentioned the important Buddhist concept of the skandhas, which is Sanskrit for "heap" or "pile." There are many layers involved with this concept. But, broadly speaking, the self as we know it consists of the following five components, which are known as the Five Skandhas:

1. Form: This refers to the physical body.

2. Feeling: We naturally seek out pleasurable sensations while rejecting unpleasant and painful sensations.

3. Thinking: We like to think. We pride ourselves on being logical and rational.

4. Activity: There is an undercurrent of thoughts that become obvious when we dream at night – even in sleep, we are not fully at rest or without activity. Actually, we cannot stop thinking at a subconscious level.

5. Consciousness: This is the awareness that we experience when we come into contact with the outside world.

Our existence is experienced through these five aspects of our ego, which are like layers of an onion. These skandhas show that the self is really very complex.

In addition to the concept of the skandhas, we will need to draw on the concept of reincarnation. As we have seen, Buddhism teaches that death is not an end; when we die, we simply change into another body. Each body is defined by the five skandhas.

After we die, most of us pass through a state called the Intermediate Skandha Body. This "body" is a temporary state that we go through between reincarnations, as we pass from one body into another.

When we are in the state of the Intermediate Skandha Body, we actually become a ghost that lives for only seven days. We may live and die seven successive lives as a temporary ghost, for up to a total of 49 days. Thus, during the 49 days after death, we have seven chances to affect our rebirth.

During this time period we get to meet with King Yama the judge and ruler of the nether world, once every seven days. Each time, the judge is presented with our records. He tabulates the good and bad deeds we have created during our lifetime, and metes out his judgment accordingly. In other words, he decides what kind of body we should take on next, depending on our past karma. Those who lived a good and decent life may have enough blessings to go to the human or heavenly realms. Those who were wicked may end up falling to the three evil paths of the hells, hungry ghosts or animals.

This Intermediate Skandha Body state is a miserable one. We are not yet accustomed to having just lost our human body. For example, we may try to lift our arms, but they feel like lead and will not move. Furthermore, everything is dark. We open our eyes wide, but cannot see a thing. And we are cold and very hungry. Worse yet, we are constantly harassed by our past creditors – people to whom we are indebted for past offenses – who wish to confuse us so that we will fall to the lower realms.

What most people fail to realize is that during this 49-day period, the actions of our surviving relatives and friends can have an immediate impact on us.

For example, in some cultures it is traditional to throw a memorial party on behalf of the deceased. In such cases it is common to drink alcohol and eat meat in memory of the departed, practices which Buddhists believe are harmful and add to the deceased's karmic debt. Buddhists also gather in honor of their loved one, and often share a meal, just without the offending elements.

Each time the deceased meets with King Yama, all the karma created in relation to the deceased is tallied up and added to his or her records. As this can happen up to seven times, there are many opportunities for the offenses created by loved ones to be added to the deceased person's record.

This is where the Buddhist customs that are still practiced by many Asians become important. Customarily, Buddhists will go back to the temple to ask for help in creating blessings for the deceased. They commission monks and nuns to recite the Buddha's name or sutras, or bow in repentance. In addition, Buddhists also know to perform various meritorious acts, including not eating meat during this time period, in order to create merit and virtue on behalf of the deceased.

If the surviving relatives and friends do meritorious deeds on behalf of the deceased during this time period, they can help him or her obtain a good body in the very next life. On the other hand, if they create offenses, say by eating meat as part of a celebration on behalf of the deceased, these offenses will worsen the fate of the dead.

In particular, this 49-day period is also the most opportune time to help the deceased obtain rebirth to the Pure Lands. Those who believe this should prepare for this transition period to maximize their rebirth chances.

For thousands of years, Mahayana Buddhism has had the tradition of providing special ceremonies for people who are dying or have recently died. In particular, the 49-Day Dharma has traditionally been of great importance for the East Asian Buddhists.

This dharma creates merit from making an offering to the Triple Jewel to help the deceased person increase their blessings and overcome the obstructions they will face during the 49-day transition period. The objective is to help the deceased person attain rebirth to the Western Bliss Pure Land right away.

But even if the deceased person is unable to reach the Pure Land immediately, the ceremony may nonetheless still help him or her ascend to the human or heavenly realms. Also, it may help them plant seeds for rebirth to the Pure Land in future lifetimes.

The 49-Day Dharma has it roots in *The Earth Store Sutra* and *The Amitabha Sutra,* as well as *The Buddha Speaks of Ullambana Sutra.* In *The Ullambana Sutra,* the Triple Jewel helps rescue Mahamaudgalyayana's mother from the realm of the hungry ghosts. How? By transferring to her all the merit generated from making offerings to the Buddhist Sangha (the community of left-home people) throughout the ten directions.

Here are a couple of anecdotes from our temple.

One disciple's beloved mother passed away a few years ago. Back then, I only taught Chan, but felt that it was important to inform my disciple about the 49-Day and Rebirth Dharmas.

His mother left him and his sister an inheritance that included a house in California, which they were in the process of selling. I therefore urged him to use some of the proceeds from the sale to pay for her Rebirth Dharmas to the Western Bliss Pure Land. I argued that even if she was not Buddhist, she should still be given the option to go to the Buddhist Pure Lands. After all, it was her money. My disciple chose the cheapest Rebirth Dharma offered at a local temple, instead of going for the more expensive, but much more effective Rebirth Dharma at another temple.

The cheaper service was more ceremonial than beneficial to the dead woman. However, because she was quite a decent Christian all of her life, she was ultimately born into the heavens.

Do you know what is sad about it? She is still upset at her favorite son for his stinginess. She has not forgiven him yet.

The second example is about a non-believer.

I have a disciple who is a dentist. His best friend is a doctor who does not believe in Buddhism. The non-believer passed away, and my dentist disciple immediately came to me to ask for help with the 49-Day Dharma.

After I agreed to his request, I asked my disciple whether his friend is rather arrogant and looks down on religion. My disciple answered in the affirmative.

How can we help people who think that what we do is nonsense or sheer superstition?

For the first three weeks, I did my normal 49-day work, but held the blessings back and asked King Yama not to apply them to the deceased doctor's account. In other words, I let him suffer for the first three weeks to increase his awareness. Eventually, he chose to go the Western Bliss Pure Land in the sixth week. Apparently, this non-believer had had enough of the suffering, and chose to enjoy the bliss of the Pure Land as soon as he was able to.

A couple of months later, my dentist disciple visited the temple, and recounted receiving a phone call from his dead doctor friend's daughter. Her dad had come back in her dreams on two consecutive nights. He told her that he was doing very well.

On the second night, he told her he must say goodbye and that he had to go. He said that he was now doing something that he had never done before: he was actually cultivating the Dharma. Why? Because, he told his daughter, he had nothing else to do but cultivate. That is what people do in the Pure Land; they no longer have the opportunity to go out and commit offenses as we do here in our world. Rather, their entire existence is geared toward practicing the Way and attaining liberation. The daughter who had this dream was unfamiliar with Pure Land Buddhism.

One significant drawback to the way that the 49-Day Dharma is usually practiced these days is that most Buddhists wait until someone dies before coming to the temple and requesting help through a 49-Day ceremony. However, according to *The Earth Store Sutra*, only 1/7th of the blessings that are generated on behalf of the deceased will actually go to the deceased. The surviving relatives will get the majority (the other 6/7th). This is one reason why most people fail to reach the Pure Land – they simply do not have enough blessings to get there.

It is understandable how some people might believe that early preparations for this 49-Day period can be construed as wishing an early death to someone. However, this is not correct and is just a superstitious belief. On the other hand, our lives are short; shouldn't we prepare ahead of time?

If you are really a believer, it is safest to prepare the 49-Day ceremony for yourself, rather than hope that your relatives will know what to do. It is not wise to let somebody else make such critical decisions for you.

It is also wise not to delay. As the Buddhists put it: The ghosts of impermanence can come at any time. More often than not, they come when we least expect it. You never know when it will be your turn.

More importantly, by requesting the 49-Day service while you are still alive, you will receive 100 percent of the blessings generated on your behalf, rather than just $1/7^{th}$. Another advantage of preparing early is that you will not impose unnecessary burdens on your relatives during the stressful time of bereavement.

If done correctly, one can dramatically improve one's rebirth through this 49-Day process.

32. Beyond The Trial

When they first learn about the trial period that most of us have to go through after death, people often ask: "I feel bad that I did not understand more about this 49-Day Dharma to request it in time for my loved ones who died years ago. Is there anything that I can do for them now that the 49-day period has already passed?"

Yes, you can still help. But it's much more involved after the 49 days are over.

First, you must generate enough blessings to allow for their rebirth to the Western Bliss Pure Land. That is no easy feat. On top of that, 49 days after their death, they were already born into a new body, in one of the six realms of rebirth. So now you must generate enough blessings to overcome obstructions to rebirth that are rooted in their present existence. The Mahayana dharma of requesting a rebirth plaque at a Buddhist temple is best suited for this goal.

I'll give you two examples to explain how this works.

There was a monk who passed away a few years ago. He was supposed to fall to the lower realms, but his family asked for help from a competent temple and he therefore was born into the heavens.

He had a wonderful time, constantly returning to visit the people he cared for deeply. They all reported feeling his presence.

However, as we have seen, to the Buddhist heavenly bliss is not the ultimate goal. When the blessings run out, we cycle back into the reincarnation wheel. To be happy with heavenly bliss is simply to be short-sighted.

Therefore, his family came to me and requested me to help him obtain rebirth to the Western Bliss Pure Land. Again, at this point, the 49-day period had passed and the monk had already been born to the heavens.

Thanks to a sincere donation made by the family, it was not long before this monk had enough rebirth blessings to make it to the Pure Land. However, it still took an additional year and half of work to persuade him to choose rebirth to the Western Bliss Pure Land. Why? I had to compete with the incredibly pleasant and blissful experiences he was having in the heavens.

There is another case that also typifies the difficulties involved in attaining rebirth after the 49-day period. A woman who had an abortion when she was younger, later came to understand more about cause and effect. She felt remorse for her act and wished to repent. Thus she decided to help her unborn child obtain rebirth to the Pure Land.

She spared no expense. She sought help from various temples. They would set up special ceremonies to help the child cross over. They dedicated special facilities on the child's behalf.

In her ongoing quest to save her unborn child, she eventually came to me and asked for help. I informed her that unfortunately the child was not doing well at all. The child was still angry at her, and yet at the same time was unable to let go of its attachment to her, because of the blood relationship.

Finally, after I was convinced of her sincerity, we were able to convince her child to go to rebirth and move on.

The 49-Day service is designed to handle the often virulent attacks that only surface after we die, as our past creditors find out that we have a chance for rebirth to the Pure Land, and therefore come at us with an eye toward vengeance while they still have the chance.

But even those who receive the 49-Day service, will also benefit from having a rebirth plaque, which will bring additional rebirth blessings and will enable the departed to cultivate more effectively and become a Buddha even sooner. Then they will have the chance to come back and save us. It is worth supporting the cultivation of those who have already made it to the Pure Land because, after all, these are the types of people who can assist you in your own cultivation and growth.

Thus, those who are sincere should consider getting rebirth plaques in addition to the 49-Day Service.

VI

Chan & Pure Land Parallel Practice: A How-To Guide

33. Reciting the Buddha's Name

In this chapter we will explain how to recite Amitabha Buddha's name, which is the basic practice of Pure Land Buddhism.

The majority of our Chan techniques will be discussed in Chapter 37. However, even the Pure Land techniques in this chapter are influenced by Chan, since the two facets of our Chan and Pure Land parallel cultivation are ultimately not separate.

There are four methods of reciting the Buddha's name:

1. Contemplating and thinking recitation: *The Contemplation Sutra* lists 16 successive contemplations.
2. Contemplating a Buddha image recitation: Select a statue of the Buddha that you like; recite the Buddha's name while contemplating it.
3. Holding the name: Keep reciting the Buddha's name to purify your mind and you can enter samadhi.
4. Real Mark Buddha recitation: Real Mark recitation is what enlightened beings do when they recite the Buddha's name.

Holding the name is by far the most widely practiced method. To practice this style of recitation, simply set aside all false-thinking and repeat Amitabha Buddha's name, either silently in your mind, or aloud.

You can recite "Emituofo," which is the Chinese pronunciation of Amitabha's name (pronounced "Ah Me Toe Fo"). However, it is also fine to use the English, "Amitabha Buddha," or any other language, such as Vietnamese, Korean, etc.

Sometimes the Sanskrit word "Namo" is added before the Buddha's name. For instance, in our Pure Land Assemblies we recite "Namo Emituofo" when we circumambulate the Buddha while doing walking recitation, and then switch to the shorter "Emituofo" for the sitting recitation.

Also, you may choose to recite in a melodic fashion, or you may use a normal speaking tone. Simply find the method of reciting that is most comfortable for you.

When we are reciting, we use the Guan Yin Dharma Door of listening to our own hearing nature. This method is described in detail in *The Shurangama Sutra*. For the purpose of our Pure Land practice, we simply need to listen with our complete attention to the sound of our own recitation. This applies even if we are not reciting aloud, but only internally. The thought of Amitabha's name in your mind still has an internal sound that you can listen to.

Or you can recite to your navel, which is known in Chinese as the *dan tian,* your spiritual center of gravity. To practice this method, just recite the Buddha's name as you place your attention on your navel.

Try not to false-think when you are reciting. In other words, your mind should not have any other thought except for the Buddha's name. Just put your full attention on the sound of your recitation. Whenever you realize that you are false-thinking, just set your thoughts aside and return to single-mindedly reciting the Buddha's name.

It is best to spend some time every day reciting in sitting and/or walking meditation. Chapter 37, "Chan Meditation Techniques," will teach you more about the mechanics of sitting meditation.

In addition, you can also recite throughout the day, whenever you are doing things that don't require conscious thinking, like washing the dishes, doing laundry, or sweeping: just stop your false-thinking, return your attention to your navel and keep reciting.

At first it may be difficult to focus inside, on your *dan tian*, while you are doing things in the external environment. However, if you keep training yourself to focus on your *dan tian*, "residing at your headquarters or central command," you will naturally become more aware of the task at hand. It's not easy, but this is the process to minimizing false-thinking when you become aware of it.

When you must think, as for example at work, then you can focus on what you are doing and stop reciting to your navel. However, when you find yourself thinking unnecessarily, then stop for a minute, return your attention to your *dan tian* and recite the Buddha's name.

Also, it is a good idea to take a break about once an hour and briefly recite to your navel. You can even set an alarm as a reminder.

The method we have described here is extraordinarily simple: try it for a while and you will quickly become adept at it. The majority of Pure Land Buddhist adherents recite the Buddha’s name all day: right after they get up in the morning, while brushing their teeth, driving to work, while at work, and so on.

You can recite the Buddha’s name anytime and anywhere. Doing so will give you energy and peace of mind. Those who are skilled can very rapidly focus on the Buddha's name, to the exclusion of all externals, enabling them to quickly recharge their batteries at will.

By practicing this method, you will see its effectiveness in calming your mind, which in turn will increase your faith in the Dharma. With faith, it is easier to enter the Buddha recitation samadhi.

Then you will be on a direct path to the Pure Land.

34. Other Methods of Pure Land Practice

How can you practice the Pure Land Dharma? The following steps will give you some guidelines:

1. Set goals

    Be certain to make the vow for rebirth to the Western Bliss Pure Land. Better yet, make sure to aim for rebirth this very lifetime.

2. Generate blessings

    It takes a tremendous amount of blessings to attain rebirth to the Pure Lands. The following chapter will explain how to plant blessings in greater detail.

    Most people fail to generate enough rebirth blessings and that is why the overwhelming majority of current Pure Land practitioners will not attain rebirth to the Pure Land at the end of this lifetime. You should be concerned that you too are among them.

    Always be on the lookout for ways to generate more rebirth blessings. Generally, any method of doing good for others will also generate blessings for you. Practicing filiality, which is the topic of Chapter 36, is one great method to generate blessings. The more blessings you have, the higher your grade of rebirth.

I teach my pupils: create great merit 立大功.

3. Observe the Precepts

Following the rules of morality outlined in the precepts will generate more rebirth blessings for you.

4. Find a teacher

Even before you accrue enough blessings to be worthy to be taught, you should always be on the lookout for a great teacher.

When you have enough blessings, a teacher will recognize it and will teach you.

Do not walk around with the attitude: "Save me, help me, teach me." Instead, be more humble and help others so as to be worthy of being helped. You can find more on the topic of Good Knowing Advisers or wise teachers in our *Chan Handbook*.

4. Build up your gongfu

Unless your cultivation gongfu (samadhi level) improves, you are on the wrong track. You should track your rate of progress. If your recitation samadhi level steadily increases, then you are gradually getting closer to the Pure Lands.

Simultaneously, as your samadhi increases, your wisdom should also unfold accordingly.

How can you tell that your wisdom is unfolding?

You become more humble. You defer to others, and let others have the limelight. You become kinder and compassionate, instead of being self-serving. You do not criticize others; rather, you patiently embrace their weaknesses and flaws. Most importantly, you no longer look at others' faults, but focus on your own.

Chapter 37: "Chan Meditation Techniques" will outline some practices to increase your samadhi power. For more detailed instructions on how to develop samadhi, consult *The Chan Handbook*.

Finally, you can also improve your concentration power by finding a good group to cultivate with regularly. If you can find a group of practitioners whose level is higher than yours, you will benefit from cultivating with them.

Many Pure Land temples have regular weekly assemblies where they get together and recite the Buddha's name. In addition, it is very beneficial to attend Fo Qi or Chan Qi retreats, special training sessions in Pure Land and Chan that last for seven days at a stretch. A typical day of recitation might begin at 4 a.m. and end at 9 p.m.

5. Request external help

Do some research, and look for competent people who can help you or your loved ones attain rebirth to Western Bliss Pure Land.

Study Pure Land Buddhism. Invest in your rebirth: Seek out help from qualified left-home people; find a good temple that can assist you during the critical 49 days after you die, to recite and perform ceremonies on your behalf. This work is designed to transfer rebirth blessings into your karmic bank account.

If you have great blessings, you will find great external help. This completes the circle: just remember to generate more rebirth blessings, continuously.

35. The Currency of Blessings

Good things happen to us because we have blessings.

Blessings are created from our meritorious and virtuous deeds. They require action, not just good intentions or promise.

Merit is created by helping others. One might assist an elderly person to cross the street, volunteer at a soup kitchen, or wash the dishes after lunch at the temple.

Virtuous deeds are acts of giving that involve taking a personal loss. Virtuous people do not mind taking a loss in order to benefit others. More importantly, virtuous acts are done solely for the sake of helping others, and not for recognition (helping oneself).

Being reborn to the Pure Land requires a tremendous amount of blessings. That is why generating rebirth blessings is a critical part of Pure Land practice.

We can compare rebirth to the Pure Land to taking a plane to a distant land. Before we can board the plane, we must have sufficient funds to pay for the ticket. Likewise, if we wish for Amitabha Buddha to greet us at the time of death and escort us to the Pure Land, we must have enough rebirth blessings to pay for this karmic transaction.

You should realize that the Western Bliss Pure Land is 10 billion worlds away from our Saha world, from this Milky Way Galaxy we live in. To give you perspective, we spend around $50 million dollars to send astronauts to the Space Station. There isn't enough money on this earth to pay for a ticket to the Western Bliss Pure Land. Therefore, you should be grateful that the Buddha taught us so many Dharma Doors to help us generate blessings.

Blessings come in two forms: those with outflows, and those without outflows. An "outflow" is a technical Buddhist term for an unwanted drain on our energy. We are riddled with these leaks, because we habitually pursue external, or outward, pleasures and engage in a non-stop stream of scattered thinking.

Blessings with outflows refer to worldly blessings such as money, fame, cars, love, etc. While these are enjoyable, they only promote outward energy flow, ultimately draining us.

In contrast, blessings without outflows, are blessings that aid in cultivating the transcendental Dharmas; these blessings help to end our outflows, so that we can control our thinking mind, and ultimately attain enlightenment.

Thus it should be clear that blessings without outflows are preferable.

Blessings with outflows are created by helping others, while hoping for rewards or gains. Blessings without outflows are created by not seeking rewards or by dedicating the merit and virtue of good actions toward the accomplishment of Buddhahood.

Higher blessings are those that are hidden. Those who are really blessed have just enough to meet their needs. For example, a high paying job, that allows you to live in luxury, is a form of withdrawal of your blessings. On the other hand, those who have just what they need will not deplete their savings by overdrawing their karmic bank account. Flaunting our assets is not a blessing, but a liability. We should learn to be very thrifty with our blessings and search for opportunities to create even more.

Those who strive to be good parents should give their children blessings, instead of money. Money spoils them; blessings help them become better people.

Blessed people tend to have fewer afflictions or suffering. This has nothing to do with material wealth; many wealthy people are not necessarily happy.

The true Buddhist does not advocate the pursuit of happiness through externals. Worldly happiness is actually a kind of suffering to the Buddhist. We live in a world of duality: happiness is defined in opposition to suffering. In happiness, suffering is built-in.

For example, people seek romantic love. It is wonderful to be able to share your life with someone special. But what begins as great love can turn into boredom or hatred: at least half of the marriages in the United States end in divorce.

Buddhism is not pessimistic; it is realistic. Those who can truly understand and behave wisely, can avoid heartache down the road.

Buddhists are not against happiness. In fact, those who are blessed, can learn ways to be happier.

How can you be happier?

You can achieve happiness by learning to do away with the things that make you suffer and seeking the permanent happiness that the Pure Lands provide. If you eliminate suffering, then all that will be left is true happiness, not the duality that is reflected in worldly happiness. While true happiness can only be attained when the cycle of birth and death has ended, prior to ending birth and death, one can still minimize suffering on this plane, and increase one's happiness.

How do you eliminate suffering? By unfolding your wisdom. Those who have wisdom will not act in ways that make other people suffer, which will in turn come around to make them suffer.

Those who have blessings will encounter a wise teacher who will teach them how to become happier.

Contrasted with worldly happiness, in the Western Bliss Pure Land, happiness is constant. There is nothing unpleasant. Everything is as you wish. The residents live in palaces and never have to work. They do not have to cook or sew because food appears as we wish; the clothes they wear are even nicer than heavenly garments. The residents of the Pure Land are so blessed that they experience no suffering whatsoever.

If you believe this, then plant blessings with greater sincerity and earnestness.

According to *The Infinite Life Sutra*, one of the major Pure Land Sutras spoken by the Buddha, those who wish to be born to the Western Bliss Pure Land should cultivate three kinds of blessings:

1. Show filial piety to, and take care of, one's parents; obey and serve one's teachers and elders; maintain a kind mind and do not kill; and practice the Ten Good Deeds (these are listed in Chapter 4, "Cause and Effect.")
2. Take refuge with the Triple Jewel; receive and maintain the precepts; and do not violate the rules of comportment.
3. Bring forth the Bodhi mind; deeply believe in cause and effect; read and recite Mahayana scriptures (from memory); and vigorously cultivate with progress.

These three groups of blessings are called pure karmas. Such pure karmas create pure blessings, which are the currency used in the Western Bliss Pure Land.

Such blessings are true wealth.

36. On Filial Piety

From the Buddhist perspective, the fundamental responsibility for human beings is to be filial, not to get a good job or become rich. Filiality in Buddhism means to pay respect to, and repay the kindness of your parents, elders, and teachers.

To practice Buddhism, one must be filial.

In previous generations (in China, in Vietnam, and in other East Asian countries) the culture was built on filiality. Buddhists believe that the strongest cultures are built on filiality. However, nowadays, even these East Asian countries are adopting Western values, and a more materialistic attitude that focuses less on family; they are forsaking their roots.

In modern society, we often don't teach our children these kinds of basic values anymore. This is why children now tend to forget to be kind to others; instead they often selfishly only do what is beneficial for them. No wonder they are not happy.

Filiality is very vast and broad, but the basic idea is to try to respect our parents and make them happy. It can be difficult to repay our parents' deep kindness, because good parents care for their children unconditionally.

Most of us are not aware of how deeply our parents care for us until we become parents ourselves. Nonetheless, we can try to make our parents happy and find opportunities to please them. If we are like that, then we set a good example for our children to be filial.

Do your best to please your parents because when you are filial to your parents, they are happy. That makes you happier. Then, not only are you and your parents happy, but the ghosts and spirits will also be happy; they will respect you. It takes wisdom to make your parents happy.

The quickest route to becoming a Buddha is to practice filial piety. Becoming a Buddha is the most important accomplishment that you can ever have in life; nothing is more important than that. All the Buddhas say, “Each and every one of you will become Buddhas.” Simply said, the sooner the better. Practicing filiality will expedite the process.

Filiality begins at home. If you know how to respect your parents, it follows that you will also know how to be filial toward the Buddha.

The ultimate and highest form of filial piety is to leave the home-life as Shakyamuni Buddha did. When you leave the home life, you no longer have parents of your own. You give up your parents so that you can become filial to all the parents of the world. This profound Buddhist wisdom is not easily understood but is very important.

Filiality to your parents comes in many forms. One of them is to plant blessings on their behalf by making offerings to the Triple Jewel, reciting mantras, bowing to the Sangha, offering meals to the Buddha and the Sangha, etc.

Whatever you offer, find the best quality you can afford and offer it sincerely.

In Western culture, people buy cards and gifts for their parents to show appreciation, particularly on Mother's and Father's Day. However, Buddhists generally don't buy gifts because it will only exhaust the recipient's blessings. Instead, make offerings to the Triple Jewel, and you will generate blessings for your parents, and yourself too.

Another form of filiality is to respect your parents. Don't tell them what to do, or that they are wrong if they don't ask for your advice. If you tell them what to do, according to Buddhism, you commit the offense of being disrespectful toward your. However, you may give them advice, if they ask for it. The ultimate subtlety is shown by waiting for the right timing.

In order to become a Buddha, one has to be a good human being. In order to be a good human being, one must practice filial piety.

The following is a guideline for how to practice filial piety toward our parents in Buddhism:

- Make offerings to your parents: give them things they need or will appreciate, and take care of them. Make sure they don't lack anything. If you can afford it, make sure your parents have enough material possessions to meet their needs, and do not to let them worry about any material lack.
- Make offerings to the Triple Jewel so that your parents don't become hungry in the future.
- Try not to make your parents feel lonely and sad. When people get old, they tend to feel like they are no longer useful to society. They can feel left

out, and that no one needs them anymore. Moreover, when you get married and have a family of your own, you can become busy taking care of your own family, and may not have time for your parents. Instead, you should give extra attention to your parents and be especially kind to them.

- Whatever you do, you should inform your parents. For example, if your parents live with you, when you go to the bank, you tell them, "I'm going to the bank." This shows that you're polite and respectful toward your parents.
- Whatever your parents do, you should be respectful, support them, and not oppose them. Support your parents according to their wishes, not your own.
- Whatever your parents ask you to do, you should do it. For example, if they ask you to go take out the trash, study, eat, sleep…etc., do it.
- Do not stop or interrupt your parents' proper activities. If they want to go to the temple, or make offerings to temples, let them continue doing so. In fact, if they can no longer drive, help them out and give them a lift!

What if your parent is a troubled person and was not a nurturing "good" parent? What if he or she had a greater share of problems and was unable to be kind or responsible? Then it behooves you to find kindness within yourself. Don't forget that this parent had a hand in bringing you into this world. At whatever level you can give to your parent, do it.

We have seen that we should all show filial piety to our parents to repay their kindness. In addition, we should also treat other elders with respect as well. Practicing filial piety will help us stay humble and become better people.

Filiality is one of the traditional, quintessential teachings from Asia, though it is also emphasized in certain other cultures. Filiality is the Buddhist way of humanity.

Finally, one must not merely talk about it; one must practice it. We can teach filial piety to our children through our actions toward our own parents, elders, teachers and ancestors. If we show filial piety, then our children will automatically do so, too.

37. Chan Meditation Techniques

Chan is the school of Buddhism that specializes in meditation.

The purpose of Chan practice is to develop our inherent wisdom and become enlightened in this lifetime. The primary approach that Chan practitioners use to open their wisdom is to develop their samadhi, or concentration power.

However, as we have seen, enlightenment is incredibly difficult to attain, and few people will be able to accomplish it in one lifetime. Nonetheless, Chan meditation techniques can benefit people on many different levels by speeding up their progress.

This is why the various schools of Buddhism all draw on the techniques of Chan. Pure Land Buddhism is no exception. In particular, if we wish to progress in our recitation skills and eventually enter the Buddha Recitation Samadhi, then we can greatly benefit from using Chan techniques for increasing our concentration.

Sitting in full-lotus is a key Chan secret. In the full-lotus posture, the left foot rests on the right thigh, and the right leg crosses over the left, with the right foot resting on the left thigh. It can take some time to be able to sit in full-lotus; however most people, unless they have a physical injury, can train themselves to do so.

For those who cannot sit in full-lotus yet, half-lotus is another option. In half-lotus, the left foot rests on top of the right thigh, and the right foot rests underneath the left leg.

Those who are not yet flexible enough to do either of the lotus postures can sit in the "easy posture." This is just the common cross-legged position, where the feet are both resting on the ground in front of you, rather than on the opposite thigh.

Regardless of which posture is used, it is best to sit flat on the ground, without the use of a round meditation cushion that elevates your hips. You can sit on a simple mat or blanket to insulate yourself from the ground.

Finally, those who are unable to sit cross-legged on the floor can also sit in a chair.

Once you have settled into your sitting posture, place your hands palm up in your lap, with the right hand on top of the left hand, with the tips of the thumbs gently touching. This is known as the Vajra Mudra.

Here are a few more general guidelines to observe during meditation:

1. Wear comfortable clothing.
2. Sit with the small of your back straight. Eventually your upper back will straighten naturally. However, it does not hurt to try and keep it straight without straining yourself.
3. Do not move during meditation. Do not scratch your nose.
4. Keep your eyes closed or one-third open. If your eyes are slightly open, your gaze should be directed downward, a couple of yards in front of you.
5. Sit facing a wall to reduce visual distractions.

6. Avoid drafts.
7. Keep your legs warm with a blanket or towel, if necessary.
8. Do not wear a hat if your head feels cold. Bear it until it naturally warms up.
9. Do not wrap a blanket around your upper body when it is cold. Instead, wear more layers; but it's best to keep yourself slightly cool. If you are too warm, it will make you drowsy.
10. Curl your tongue up to gently touch the gums behind your upper front teeth. This closes an important meridian to make the Qi (energy) flow better.
11. Swallow the saliva that collects.

To practice the Pure Land method while sitting, simply cross your legs and recite the Buddha's name to your navel, as described in Chapter 33.

It is best if you meditate daily. Those who are serious about their cultivation should sit an hour a day. It may take some time to build up being able to sit for an hour without uncrossing your legs. However, the longer you can sit, especially in full-lotus, the more you will increase your samadhi and the more effective your recitation will be.

To sit for this long, you will need to learn how to manage the pain in your legs and back. The leg pain can be especially intense if you are in full-lotus.

A good way to build up your capacity to endure the pain is to start out sitting for as long as you are able. Then use a timer, and sit for two minutes longer every day. This way you will gradually increase your ability to sit through the pain.

This may not be what you expected (or wanted!) to hear. Indeed, most other styles of meditation will encourage you to sit as comfortably as possible, and will only talk about pleasant states and relaxation.

However, sitting through the pain is one of the key Chan secrets for increasing concentration. The good news is that, if you work hard, you can easily begin to make progress with this method.

In fact, there are many advantages to facing pain in your meditation. For more details consult our *Chan Handbook*.

Briefly speaking, enduring the leg pains not only reduces our false-thinking and increases concentration, but it also trains us to be more patient, and it improves the Qi flow throughout the whole body. Since illnesses are caused by blockages in our body's Qi flow, when we meditate, we actually can heal ourselves, especially if we are willing to cultivate intensely.

If you wish to recite the Buddha's name during walking meditation, place your hands in the same Vajra Mudra position that is used in sitting, at the level of your navel, with the thumbs touching. Look at the ground a few yards ahead of you. Do not look around. Place your attention at your *dan tian* and listen to the sound of your own recitation. You can also recite while you are walking about normally, throughout the day.

The use of Chan Meditation techniques, such as full-lotus, is an important part of the parallel practice of Chan and Pure Land. This parallel practice is designed to maximize our rebirth chances to the Western Bliss Pure Land, by both developing our own samadhi power, and by riding on Amitabha Buddha's power to help us.

In addition, if we recite the Buddha's name, there is no need to contemplate a topic. Instead, we only need to take the Buddha's name as if it were a raft being used to cross the ocean. We dare not let go of it, even for a brief instant. Our mouth recites and our mind focuses. Each syllable originates from the mind and is enunciated by the mouth. Our mind is clear and bright, not murky and not scattered.

There are also two more analogies that are relevant here. First, to recite the Buddha's name is like a cat watching a mouse. With completely focused attention, its spirit is totally aroused and its hair stands on end. Secondly, reciting the Buddha's name is like a chicken hatching its eggs. The hen focuses totally on the act of hatching, to the exclusion of everything else, oblivious to thirst or hunger. If we can recite with this kind of concentration, although it is a form of phenomenon recitation, not only can we be assured of rebirth, but we are also bound to awaken to the principles as well. As Kong Gu Chan Master said, "There is no need to investigate who is reciting the Buddha's name. Directly strive for becoming single-minded and one day you will be enlightened."

Moreover, if we can recite the Buddha's name and meditate, then it can truly be called Pure Land and Chan parallel cultivation. We are not neglecting phenomenon or noumenon recitation. Rather, it is like riding a boat to the West, in that we rely both on rowing with oars (Chan) as well as wind power (recitation).

As Chan Master Yong Ming Shou said, "With Pure Land and Chan together, it's like a tiger with horns: in this life, one is a teacher of men and, in the future, one will become a patriarch."

VII

Closing Thoughts

38. "I'll Be Back!"

Some people feel that they could not possibly go to the Pure Land because that is just too selfish.

For example, many women, especially from Asian cultures, are conditioned to believe that they will fall short of their duty to their family if they do not make extreme sacrifices to care for them, such as forgoing marriage and personal happiness. But for how long must they continue to make these sacrifices; isn't one lifetime long enough?

Moreover, although we might have the best of intentions, we are limited in how much we can help our loved ones when we ourselves are still confused.

Only when we attain real understanding can we truly help others. Otherwise, we often create more confusion through our bad advice, and become more of a burden by injecting ourselves into other people's problems.

More specifically, before we help others, we must develop transcendental wisdom. In other words, we should first reach the level of an Arhat, or preferably higher.

But sadly, very few of us will be able to attain such lofty achievements in this lifetime.

This brings us to another wonderful aspect of the Pure Land Dharma Door: if we first go to the Western Bliss Pure Land

and study under Amitabha Buddha, we can have faith that he will then guide us how to best rescue our loved ones.

Typically once we are in the Pure Land, we will not return to this Saha world until we have the skills and wisdom to save those with whom we have karmic affinities.

However, under special circumstances and the right conditions, Amitabha might send us back, even though we may not personally be ready yet.

For example, you might come back early in order to help your loved ones locate a competent teacher who can save them or send them to the Pure Land. Once your task in the Saha world is done, then you yourself will return to the Pure Land to continue your cultivation there.

These kinds of cases occur more often than people realize. This is because the Pure Land Dharma Door is a Mahayana approach to liberation, and the aim of Mahayana is to save all living beings as soon as possible. Therefore, chances are that "special operations" missions, such as described above, are actually a common part of cultivation in the Pure Land.

All of this is only possible because Amitabha Buddha is watching over us.

Simply have faith that he will help us fulfill our wishes.

In brief, we should focus on two things:

1. By all means, make sure to be reborn in the Pure Land at the end of this very life time.

2. Before you leave, make vows to save those who you wish to help in the future. Eventually, when

conditions are ripe, Amitabha Buddha will guide you to fulfill those vows.

Homage to Amitabha Buddha of the Western Pure Land!

Homage to Amitabha Buddha of the Western Pure Land!

Homage to Amitabha Buddha of the Western Pure Land!

39. A Path Toward Goodness

Buddhism, like many of the major world religions, can be seen as a path toward goodness.

In Buddhism, we regard the Buddha as having reached perfect goodness. Pure Land Buddhism is unique in that it offers an easier path for people of all capacities to reach this state of perfect goodness, and become Buddhas themselves.

As we progress toward this goal, we should count our blessings. We are fortunate to have been born with human bodies, which are very difficult to attain. We are also fortunate to have encountered the Mahayana Dharma, and should make the most of our opportunity.

The following tale illustrates the rarity of this opportunity.

The Buddha once was walking with Ven. Ananda, his attendant, in the forest. He scooped up a handful of dirt and asked Ven. Ananda: “Is there more dirt in the great earth or in my hand?”

“Of course, World Honored One, the great earth has more earth,” replied Ananda.

“So it is! So it is!” said the Buddha. “The number of living beings who obtain a human body is like the amount of earth in the palm of my hand. In contrast, the number of living beings who lose their human bodies is the same as the amount of dirt on the great earth."

Furthermore, it is difficult to encounter Mahayana, let alone the Mahayana Pure Land Dharma. And even once we encounter the Dharma, it is still very hard to successfully cultivate and become enlightened. And the ultimate goal of reaching Buddhahood is much more difficult to attain than enlightenment.

Thus we should be thankful for the Pure Land teachings, which provide us with a shorter and more direct path to Buddhahood. We should vigorously develop our faith, vows and practice, so that we can take advantage of this wonderful Dharma Door and attain rebirth to the Pure Land, where we will never again have to suffer, and we will experience a most wonderful life dedicated to cultivation.

In conclusion, recall that faith, vows, and practice are the three requisites of the Pure Land Dharma:

1. Faith: One should have faith:

    - Especially in the Buddha's wisdom and vow power
    - In oneself: we are very blessed to encounter this Mahayana Pure Land Dharma
    - That the Pure Land Dharma can help us quickly escape birth and death

2. Vows: then one should make vast vows:

    - To marshal resources
    - To control one's destiny
    - Such vows act as a lifeline, lifetime after lifetime

3. Practice:

    - To vigorously practice to certify to the faith
    - To improve the rebirth grade
    - To develop the recitation samadhi
    - To help others

If we can properly cultivate the Pure Land Dharma, we can prepare for a good rebirth in our next life, and also experience great benefits in this lifetime.

Initially, our motivation for reaching the Pure Land is, and should be, to relieve our own suffering. Ultimately, however, the Pure Land is a training ground for Bodhisattvas. After we have attained wisdom there, we can come back to the impure lands to benefit other living beings.

The Pure Lands are not the end of the road.

The true spirit of Mahayana is that each one of us, by perfecting our skills, can eventually become a Buddha. This is truly the greatest accomplishment that anyone can attain. And it is something that each one of us is capable of doing.

Once we reach Buddhahood, we will have realized perfect enlightenment. Then we can return to impure lands, like our Saha world, and rescue countless living beings, ferrying them across the turbulent sea of birth and death, to the other shore: the permanent bliss of Nirvana.

VIII

Appendix

Questions and Answers

This section contains a collection of questions and concerns that can help clarify misunderstandings about Pure Land Buddhism.

Non-Buddhists and the Pure Land

Question:

Must people be Buddhist to obtain rebirth to the Western Bliss Pure Land?

Answer:

Not at all.

Amitabha Buddha does not discriminate between Buddhists and non-Buddhists. Many non-Buddhists have already obtained rebirth.

Do not believe rumors you may hear that you must keep precepts or have samadhi power or wisdom before you are worthy for rebirth. Just accrue rebirth blessings through the three requisites of the Pure Land practice and you'll have a good chance.

Evil People and the Pure Land

Question:

How is it possible for evil people to obtain rebirth to the Pure Lands?

Answer:

They can, if they accrued enough blessings in previous lives to counter the evil they commit in this lifetime.

Is this fair? Yes, it is. One should not be punished for a lifetime of evil if all of one's prior lifetimes were spent doing good.

Incidentally, the Pure Lands are perfect for the most evil people. Let's send them all there.

Why? There will be less suffering in this world if evil people are reborn into the Pure Lands; once they attain some wisdom, then they will stop their pattern of doing evil and harming others. It's not such a bad "punishment" for evil people to be reborn where they can only become good!

Help for the Deceased Beyond the 49-day Period

Question:

What can we do for those who have been dead for more than 49 days?

Answer:

You can get them a rebirth plaque.

Although it is less ideal to provide them rebirth assistance after the 49-day period, as it is during that period in which the deceased have the chance to choose their next body, we still can help generate rebirth blessings for them.

This is like making deposits of rebirth blessings to their account. It does take a bit longer because, in addition to needing blessings for rebirth, they also need blessings to overcome the obstructions resulting from their current body. When they have enough blessings, they can obtain rebirth to the Western Bliss Pure Land.

Help for Elderly and Sick Relative

Question:

How can I help my elderly and sick grandfather?

Answer:

You could do the following, depending on your resources:

Request a Medicine Master Buddha plaque for him to help relieve his pain and suffering.

Request a 49-day service for him. If you can request it before he passes away, you will maximize its effectiveness.

Request a rebirth plaque to accrue his rebirth blessings now.

Dreaming of Relatives in a Bad State

Question:

I often dream of my deceased aunt in a sad state. What can I do for her?

Answer:

This is explained in *The Earth Store Sutra.* Deceased relatives sometimes manage to appear in our dreams to ask for help. That is all the blessings they can muster: to let us know of their state of misery. We should be compassionate and help create blessings on their behalf to relieve their suffering.

If you can afford it, get her a rebirth plaque to send her to the Western Bliss Pure Land.

Proof of Rebirth

Question:

What proof do you have that people have obtained rebirth to the Pure Lands?

Answer:

The Chinese have plenty of records dating back thousands of years about people who have obtained rebirth from all walks of life.

It is not our job to try to convince you. Religion is a personal matter. We do not believe that we have to try to convert everyone. We do not discriminate between Buddhists and non-Buddhists.

We suggest that you have faith in the words of the Buddhas and Bodhisattvas. But we have no problem if you do not believe.

I do hope that you find it worthwhile to invest in your rebirth chances, just in case it is true. People spend a lot more on frivolous things such as fancy cars, boats and other things they don't really need.

If you are blessed enough, you will.

My Religion Forbids Investigating Buddhist Dharmas

Question:

What if my religion forbids me to look into the Buddhist Dharmas?

Answer:

Then do not look. You have to live with your conscience. I can't advise you to go against your conscience.

But if you are allowed to use your head at all, you should try to keep an open mind.

I like to live my life in freedom. I have profound respect for each individual. I respect them enough to support them in their choices.

If my Buddhist disciples wish to seek or follow another religious faith, they are most welcome at any time. Why? I hope to be on good terms with them, so that they come back and save me if they find a better path.

I hope that you will not force your children down the same path that you took. If you love them at all, let them choose for themselves. Live and let live.

Buddhism's Nationality

Question:

Does Pure Land have a nationality? Is it Vietnamese or Chinese Pure Land?

Answer:

It is neither.

I am Vietnamese and I practiced under Chinese and Vietnamese masters. I explain Buddhism in English with translation into the various languages. Most of our lectures are translated into Vietnamese and Chinese.

I speak in English to repay the generosity and kindness of the American people for supporting my practice. I hope to make my Dharma available in Chinese and Vietnamese in order to repay my late teachers' kindness and compassion.

We have followers who speak Japanese, Korean, Spanish, French and other languages.

Buddhism knows no national or political boundaries. It is important to be cognizant that each tradition of Buddhism has its unique strengths and advantages.

Being American, I prefer to pick out and learn from the best of each tradition, be it Taiwanese or Cambodian or Russian. I want to learn from the best and will not settle for less. This is the kind of Mahayana that we propagate.

Developing the Ability to Recite the Buddha's Name

Question:

How can I increase my recitation ability?

Answer:

If you mean how you can increase your recitation samadhi, then you need the proper methodology.

You can't expect to do well unless you have the proper technique, just as you need an excellent recipe to produce the tastiest dish.

The important thing is to find a competent teacher. He will do a lot more for you than you realize, least of which is to make sure that you make progress with your practice.

Good teachers never waste your time.

Specializing

Question:

Most teachers recommend that we specialize in reciting the Buddha's name, i.e. practice Pure Land. Why do you advocate both Pure Land and Chan?

Answer:

We use the Chan training techniques in order to improve the recitation skills of our students. It seems to work pretty well.

The advanced Chan training techniques seem to help those students with higher potential progress a lot more quickly over the years.

If you understand both Chan and Pure Land, then you will see that they are really one and the same. Until you understand, follow the instructions and eventually you'll get there.

Too Young to Practice Pure Land

Question:

Would you recommend Pure Land to young people?

Answer:

Yes. I'd recommend it to people of all ages.

An American disciple of mine has a first cousin who lives in Southeast Asia. He was only 23 years old when his neighbor's car ran into his motor-bike and killed him.

Here in the United States, I have met families who have relatives who die unexpectedly when they are in their 30s and in the prime of life.

As we Buddhists say: the ghost of impermanence can come at any time.

My disciples have even invested in rebirth plaques for their children who are barely 3 years old.

Abstain from Eating the Five Pungent Plants

Question:

Should we abstain from onion and garlic?

Answer:

Yes.

Doing so will go a long way toward improving your recitation practice.

In fact, left-home people who are serious about helping others obtain rebirth to the Western Bliss Pure Land, should be careful to avoid eating the pungent plants: onion, spring onions, garlic, leeks, shallots, and other such members of the onion and garlic families because they are detrimental to our effectiveness.

Aiding Recitation for the Deceased

Question:

Is it a good thing to participate in aiding recitation sessions, where groups of practitioners recite for those who have recently died?

Answer:

It is a very nice tradition and gesture that people want to help those who are deceased with their rebirth chances. But it is fraught with problems, particularly because doing so means that we are directly meddling in others' business.

Few people realize that the deceased is subject to attacks from his past creditors who do not wish for him to escape. Here we are meddling in the debt settlement. How would you feel if you were the creditors?

Monks and nuns who are trained in helping the deceased by performing rebirth mantras and prayers and in generating rebirth blessings are professionals in this regard. These efforts constitute meddling but through their training they are equipped to handle this and they have some level of protection which the common person doesn't. If you choose to meddle by joining these aiding recitation groups, you should be aware that it carries consequences: you may be subject to retaliation.

I hope that your temple takes measures to protect you against potential retaliation from the creditors. If they don't, you may be in danger. How do you know if they do? You shouldn't have to ask.

They should inform you and tell you the dos and don’ts of it when you participate. If they fail to do so, then chances are that they can’t protect you.

Practicing Pure Land Buddhism By Oneself

Question:

One of the major objectives of the Pure Land practice is to obtain rebirth. Isn't it better to stay at home, concentrate on the practice and minimize contamination from others?

Answer:

No. If you want to practice Pure Land, you must learn the proper techniques. You are better off with proper guidance from a competent teacher.

I advise you not to practice by yourself until your teacher advises you to.

I advocate the Great Assembly Dharma: a special and wonderful training technique used at our temple. It is far better than practicing by yourself.

Finally, practice is good. Continued progress in your practice is better.

A monk, who is a Dharma brother of mine, just wanted to cultivate. His family bought him a small house in the desert so that he could practice without any disruptions. He has been doing it for four years now, and has made no progress whatsoever. In fact, he's regressing somewhat because his ego has grown, and he refuses to listen to others.

Depending on Others' Help

Question:

Some are lazy. They wish for rebirth to the Western Bliss Pure Land. They get a rebirth plaque to accrue rebirth blessings. Wouldn't that make them complacent, and not take reciting the Buddha's name seriously, because they think that they can't make much difference?

Answer:

That should not happen if the rebirth blessings generated are of high quality.

As rebirth blessings accrue to significant levels, the beneficiaries will change for the better. If not, it would not hurt to consider a change of venues.

Unfortunately for you, there are no rating agencies. I would not trust any type of rating in these rebirth matters because people who understand, never rate others.

Wishing Only to Recite the Buddha's Name

Question:

I practice reciting the Buddha's name. If I also bow repentances, recite sutras, maintain mantras etc., would that be counter-productive? Would that not cause discontinuity in my recitation and make it difficult to become single-minded?

Answer:

Not at all. Your problem is not what you should do; it is how you do it.

There is no high or low in the Pure Land practices. You cannot tell which Dharma Door is best suited to you. Your Good Knowing Adviser is in a better position to tell you what to specialize in.

Practicing Pure Land Buddhism is not merely reciting the Buddha's name alone. This is a common misunderstanding for self-taught Buddhist practitioners who only learn from books. They all seem to think that they need to specialize in one Dharma Door, so that they can become single-minded.

What the books fail to mention is that you are not supposed to specialize in one particular practice until your Good Knowing Adviser tells you to!

Helping Parents Deceased Over 30 Years Ago

Question:

Our parents passed away more than 30 years ago. If we get rebirth plaques for them, how would that help them if they have been reborn as humans [who are unable to cultivate the Dharma]? Would it help them if they do not know how to cultivate or believe in Buddhism? What if they fell into the three evil paths, what should we do?

Answer:

Getting rebirth plaques for them is like opening a savings account so that rebirth blessings can be periodically deposited. When the rebirth blessings are adequate, then they will obtain rebirth when conditions are favorable.

You can also dedicate the merit from your cultivation to them, but if you really want to help, then rebirth plaques are the way to go. This will enable you to enlist “professional help” from left-home people who have been trained to make a difference.

There is no guarantee. You just have to find the best possible way to help them. Be satisfied with trying your best to help. At least, you can do something for them. Do it while you still can. For example, animals cannot do much for their parents!

The more offerings you make, the sooner they’ll obtain rebirth.

Can Homosexuals Obtain Rebirth?

Question:

Can gay people enter the Pure Lands?

Answer:

Yes, they can.

The Buddhas do not discriminate as we do. They will welcome anyone who has enough blessings to make it to their lands.

I would add that they will be much happier in the Pure Lands, too.

Homosexual Buddhists

Question:

Can gay people become Buddhists?

Answer:

Yes. They, too, have the Buddha nature and can attain Buddhahood. The most direct path to Buddhahood is to become Buddhist and observe the precepts.

Reciting Aloud or Silently?

Question:

One monk told me that reciting the Buddha's name loudly has the most merit. Another monk told me that reciting the Buddha's name silently is more meritorious. Who is right?

Answer:

Neither is.

One of your major objectives is to practice the Buddha's recitation. It does not matter how you go about achieving it. If reciting loudly helps you concentrate better, then you should definitely do that. On the other hand, silent recitation might work better, perhaps when you are tired or you're getting hoarse.

Follow-up Question:

Allow me to clarify for you. They are not my teachers.

Answer:

You still seem attached to the mark of being your teacher or not being your teacher.

Troubles & Difficulties

Question:

I have lived a decent life. Why is it that I still have so many troubles and difficulties?

Answer:

These difficulties are karmic debts from prior lives. This is why wise people fear planting bad causes, while confused people only fear unwanted results.

Victim of War

Question:

If there is a direct relationship between cause and effect, then why did I suffer the consequences of war, though I did not want to go to war, or choose to do so?

Answer:

There are two kinds of retributions:

1. Proper retribution: only you yourself endure the consequences.
2. Common retribution: a group must endure the consequences of mass karmic action such as war or famine.

When we are distressed by conflict or hostility that we perceive from individuals or groups such as political parties, corporations, and social organizations, we must stop blaming them and find common ground with them.

We must learn to work together and function harmoniously, instead of insisting that we are the only ones who are right. We are mutually interconnected.

Against Progress

Question:

In order to make progress, we need to work hard, and fight for it. Buddhism seems to be too passive. Is the Buddha against progress?

Answer:

Buddha is not against progress. He is only against progress at the price of enslaving oneself, or destroying others. Progress is desirable when it is gained constructively. There is no real progress if it involves slavery, or ruthlessness in the pursuit of our goals.

Why do Meditation Students not Recite Buddha's Name?

Question:

I understand that one of the goals of cultivation is to avoid the catastrophe of falling into the three evil paths. Why is it that Chan cultivators do not recite the Buddha's name?

Answer:

I cannot answer for them. You'll have to ask them yourself.

I can however tell you how I feel about it.

When we cultivate, we should be careful not to become overly confident.

Unless Chan students are certain that they will become enlightened this lifetime, they are all better off reciting the Buddha's name and seeking rebirth to the Pure Land at the end of this very lifetime.

Yes, those who have some potential and who are willing to truly work hard can strive for enlightenment in this lifetime. But we have already discussed how difficult it is to succeed at this goal, and there are never any guarantees. Therefore, I would recommend getting insurance against failure by reciting the Buddha's name.

Other Irreversibility Expedients

Question:

We can recite Amitabha's name to obtain irreversibility. Are there any other expedients?

Answer:

Once we get to the Pure Land, we will obtain irreversibility. Therefore, the Pure Land School has many Dharmas to help you obtain rebirth other than reciting the Buddha's name; for instance, one may practice bowing repentances, maintaining rebirth mantras, making transferences to adorn the Pure Land, reciting sutras, etc…

Strange Manifestations While Reciting Buddha's Name

Question:

When reciting the Buddha's name in the evening, I often notice strange manifestations. Can you tell me why?

Answer:

That is probably from the invisible beings.

Reciting the Buddha's name is very beneficial to the beings in the area. Therefore they might come to show their gratitude to your helping them plant seeds of rebirth.

For instance, there was someone who a few abortions. She often felt ill at ease as if being harassed mentally. She often heard strange noises. When she turned on our Buddha recitation audio file, the noises would immediately stop. At times she felt as if someone was stroking her arms. If she spoke aloud, telling them to behave in order to receive our help for rebirth, they would stop causing trouble.

It is not uncommon for invisible beings to manifest phenomena to draw our attention when they wish to ask for help in attaining rebirth and ending their miseries.

Abortion

Question:

I had an abortion. When reciting the Earth Store Sutra, what do I need to do to transfer the merit and virtue to my child?

Answer:

Aborted babies experience great suffering and still hang around their parents because:

1. They love their parents
2. They also hate their parents because of their cruel act

Therefore, you need to generate blessings to help them obtain liberation from their misery.

Reciting the Earth Store Sutra is very beneficial for the baby. You should recite the Sutra three times and transfer the merit and virtue to the baby. This tends to create help to get the baby out of the Three Evil Paths.

Better yet, you should also consider requesting a rebirth plaque from a Mahayana temple to help the baby get reborn to the Pure Land with Amitabha Buddha instead of continuing to revolve in the Wheel.

Using Recitation Beads While Talking

Question:

I often use the recitation beads while listening to the sutra lectures or talking to other people. Is that proper?

Answer:

Recitation beads are excellent tools to remind us to be mindful of the Buddha's name.

However, you should not imitate others and use the recitation beads mindlessly.

The proper method of using the recitation beads is that, each time you move one bead, you recite the Buddha's name once. Gradually, your recitation becomes automatic. This is different from merely physically moving the beads without reciting or being mindful of the Buddha's name, like most people do.

Therefore, if you do it right, you can use the recitation beads while listening to lectures or talking with others.

Personally, I do not like to use the recitation beads because it reveals that I am reciting the Buddha's name: that might be construed as advertising oneself.

I prefer to practice in a low-key fashion and avoid drawing attention to myself. Real cultivation is to blend in with others while practicing.

Using Recitation Beads

Question:

How should I use the recitation beads, especially when I get to the top bead?

Answer:

Recitation beads can be used between the thumb, index finger and middle finger as per the enclosed pictures.

When you get to the special bead on top, there is no need to do anything special. One should stop differentiating the beads when reciting the Buddha's name.

If you have real gongfu, then even if the Buddha comes, you would not pay attention or get excited.

Practice reciting the Buddha's name without any type of discrimination; this will make it much easier for you to enter the Buddha Recitation Samadhi.

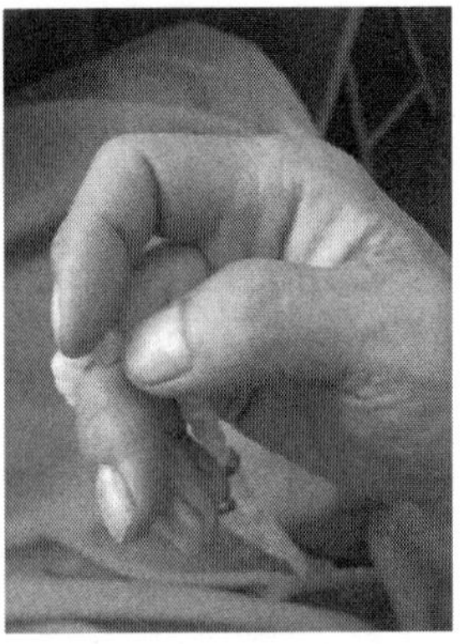

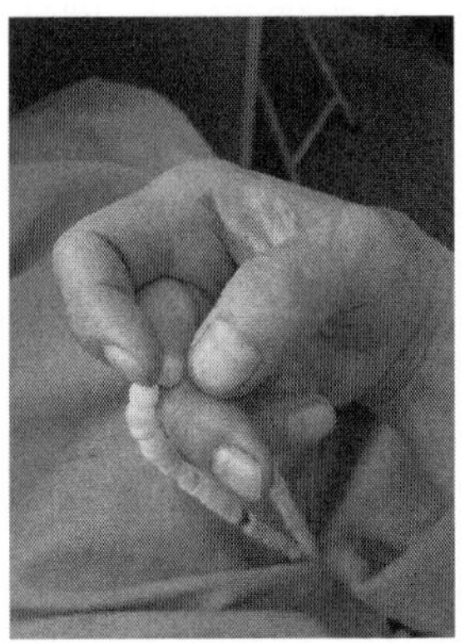

Past Creditors

Question:

Is it correct to assume that external wounds are the results of past offenses?

When I concentrate on reciting the Buddha's name, I encounter many obstructions. I was advised to accord with conditions and transfer the merit and virtue to my past creditors. What is the appropriate course of action?

Answer:

Correct! Getting hurt is the retribution for past karmas.

When reciting the Buddha's name, or when cultivating in general, one will encounter obstructions and difficulties. The tests can come in a few forms:

1. Karmic obstructions: For example the nature of your work is not easy to perform.
2. Retribution obstructions: For example, you obstructed someone's cultivation in the past, now he comes to obstruct you as payback. This case is generally referred to as obstructions from one's past creditors.
3. Affliction obstructions: Even though the obstructions and difficulties are no big deal, you nonetheless feel that they are a big deal, get very afflicted, and quit.

I am not clear of what is meant by "according with conditions," in this context. You should clarify it with the person who told this to you.

When encountering obstructions or resistance, you should patiently endure it instead of complaining or getting afflicted. How can you make progress without learning to resolve problems? Can you earn a diploma without passing the test?

A Good Knowing Adviser can teach or help you learn how to deal with obstructions in order to make progress. At each level, cultivators will encounter different types of obstructions which require specific counter measures and cannot be generalized.

49 Days for Christians

Question:

Hi:

I am a devout Christian.

My mother recently passed away and I am very interested in your Buddhist concept of the 49-day period.

What can I do to help my dear mother who wishes to be near God?

Answer:

My condolences.

The Buddhist teachings about the 49-day period explains what happens to most people after death.

During the 49-days after your mother's death, you can help her cause of obtaining a better life, by drawing near your God and making donations on her behalf. For example, you could donate money to charity or to help build a new wing for your church.

That will go a long way toward helping her future life and getting what she wishes.

Best wishes.

Buddhas Before Amitabha?

Question:

Emituofo! Greetings to you, Master. I have been pondering about this for a long time. Please help clarify it for me.

Ven. Master, in Buddhism, which Buddhas became Buddhas before Amitabha? Please kindly instruct me.

Emituofo.

Answer:

Countless Buddhas became Buddhas before Amitabha.

Why should that matter to you?

The most important consideration for you should be what to do this lifetime in order to quickly become a Buddha yourself.

Eating Meat & Reciting the Buddha's Name

Question:

Ven. Master!

Please help clarify for me the following:

1. I have been reciting the Buddha's name for quite a while, but because of scheduling conflicts from work, I have not been able to do it at specific times. Usually, I recite the Buddha's name all the time everywhere: whether it be while walking or working with my hands. I wonder whether or not such recitations would be beneficial at all because I fear that I have been calling out to him instead of reciting his name.

2. Often while I eat meat and fish I would recite his name: am I committing offenses? My question is if I recite the Buddha's name but I am not a vegetarian, would I be committing offenses?

I hope that you would kindly instruct me.

Answer:

Thank you for sharing your concerns with us.

1. You are doing just fine by reciting the Buddha's name whenever you can during the day. It would be more beneficial to recite his name with utmost respect and faith because his name represents the kindest and most wholesome thought that your mind can formulate.

2. There is no offense in reciting the Buddha's name while eating. After you become more adept at it, you will naturally lose desire for meat and fish because your mind will become more compassionate and pure.

Getting Sick from Reciting Buddha's Name for Others

Question:

Master:

Our Way place has many members. That is why we often have to participate and recite on behalf of the members' deceased family and relatives.

Does reciting continuously for 8 hours really help?

Each time I go, I'd fall sick. Is it because of the excessive yin qi?

What can we do to avoid having problems when we recite for others? We can't say no.

Answer:

The more you recite the better it is because more merit and virtue is created on behalf of the deceased. There is really no magic regarding the 8 hours. What's important is to create blessings within the 49 days period.

If you choose to provide recitation assistance then you must be prepared to pay for the consequences of meddling into other's affairs.

I wish that lay people would be more careful and not get involved in these types of recitation assistance ceremonies. This is a big deal and requires the guidance of left-home people. More importantly, sanghans who really understand the seriousness of this spiritual process will automatically shield you because they are asking you to get involved in other's affairs which will result in karmic retribution. If left-home people ask you to go help recite without explaining to you the consequences or offering to shield you, then you should reconsider your involvement.

If you feel that you cannot refuse their requests then you should ask yourself whether you are really helping at all?

It's much better to respectfully refuse their misplaced trust on you. Explain to them the critical junction that the deceased is facing and advise them to seek effective help instead of opting for a "show" for the living family, which is not of much help to the deceased. Passing on the request for assistance to those who are qualified, is much better than submitting to their uninformed wishes.

Only Wish to Recite Buddha's Name & Bow

Question:

Ven. Master:

I hope that you will instruct me because I do not know much about Buddhism.

In the morning, I would like to bow to the Buddha for 15 minutes but do not wish to recite the Sutras. Can I only recite the Buddha's name and bow to the Buddha?

Thank you for your instructions.

Answer:

You are doing just fine.

I would suggest the following minor considerations:

1. Please listen to audio files on the Proper Dharma. For example, listen while driving to work: that will naturally help you get more exposure to Mahayana while minimizing for your false thinking. In particular, you should listen to all of my late teacher's Dharma Talk audio files because they are very insightful.

2. Make sure to dedicate the merit and virtue of your daily cultivation as per the following link to our web site:
   http://www.chanpureland.org/2012/06/1870/

If you do the above, you will eventually enjoy bowing and reciting the Buddha's name a lot more. And naturally, you will also like reciting Sutras such as the Small Amitabha Sutra. Keep up the good work!

Committing Evil Karma Near the Time of Death

Question:

Ven. Master,

Emituofo!

May I ask: if one recites the Buddha's name one's whole life, aspiring to obtain rebirth to the Western Bliss Pure Land, but at the time of death, evil karmas arise, can one still obtain rebirth?

Please kindly instruct us for the sake of all living beings.

Also, if while alive, one knows nothing about the Buddha Recitation Dharma Door, nor does one believe in the Triple Jewel, however at the time of death, one encounters a Good Knowing Adviser, and one manages to drop everything and single-mindedly recites the Buddha's name, and good karmas arise, is it possible to obtain rebirth?

Answer:

I am not sure why you ask these types of questions when you can already find answers from books. You should consult the Pure Land books for the typical answers. However, as per your request, I'll provide a few insights.

1. The critical point is what happens at the time of death. If you encounter heavy karmic obstructions, even if you led a wholesome life, it is most unlikely that you will obtain rebirth. Such is the nature of karmic obstructions: you cannot overcome them.

2. The Pure Land books would tell you that in the case you describe, yes, you are likely to obtain rebirth to the Pure Land. I believe it is because of the aid you will receive from your Good Knowing Adviser at this crucial moment; very rarely is it because of your own last minute recitation. Furthermore, if you are not a believer, what are the chances that you will encounter such a savior from Buddhism? Therefore, this person's chance for rebirth is even slimmer than in the first case.

You should understand that the most direct and easiest way to attain liberation is through the Pure Land Dharma Door. This is because one can obtain rebirth to the Pure Land if one can get the proper help. More specifically, if you have blessings with the Pure Land Dharma Door, either through accrual during the current lifetime or from prior lifetimes, you can encounter a monk or nun who is able to assist with your rebirth.

Finally, I am sorry to sound like a contrarian but from my 20-year experience with Mahayana I have learned that it is near impossible to obtain rebirth to the Pure Land through one's own efforts. This is because I have seen too many people fail. In other words, if you are told that it is quite easy to obtain rebirth to the Pure Land, you should seek a second opinion!

Religious Faith

Question:

Venerable Master:

I am faced with a very serious conflict. My dad is a believer of the Cao Đài faith, while my mom is Buddhist.

When I was young, I used to go to a Cao Đài temple to make contributions. Occasionally, I would also follow my mother to the temple to bow to the Buddhas. As I grew older, I no longer frequented the Cao Đài temple and would accompany my mother to the Buddhist temple on mid-month days of the lunar months.

In my dreams, I often see myself flying in the sky, walking on water or the tips of grass blades. At times, I would dream that I was at the Cao Đài temple but it was as if I was an invisible presence because no one paid attention to me. I would hang out there but never could participate in any full ceremony. Sometimes, I would dream of the Buddha and GuanYin Bodhisattva: I would then kneel in front of them and recite the Buddha's name.

Now, I wish to take refuge with the Triple Jewel but my mother would not hear of it and wants me to follow my dad's faith. While I have faith in both religions, I still prefer to be Buddhist.

Please kindly advise me. What I should do?

Thank you very much!

Answer:

My teacher, the late patriarch, Ven. XuanHua, says that all religions are not outside of Buddhism.

That is because:

1. Fundamentally, all religious faiths advocate goodness. All the goodness that are taught in other religions are encompassed in the Buddhist goodness.

2. Buddhism is all-compassing.

3. The Great Master no longer discriminates.

Since you are not yet non-discriminating, I'll propose the following:

1. It is very good to have a religious faith. It provides balance in life. For example, Catholics go to church on Sundays because it helps them touch base with the inherent goodness in them instead of spending that time plotting to serve their insatiable egos.

2. Since you are still living at home, it is not advisable to go against your parents' wishes. If you feel that strongly about acting on your religious beliefs, why should you even become Cao Đai at all? Just keep the status quo since both your parents are OK with it.

3. You could become Buddhist after you move out of the house and assert your independence financially. There is no rush, is there? As long as you stay on the good side, then you are acting like a Buddhist already. The Buddhist practices discreetly: they do not advertise themselves.

4. Once you've asserted your independence then it's time for you to begin to gently tell your parents about your desire to not ever force religious faith on your children and that you will respect their choice for religion.

5. Make sure that your potential spouse respects your personal faith. Those who have little respect for religions are not good mates in the long haul. Most of them make for very poor parents as well because they are not good role models for the next generation.

How to Make Vows

Question:

Ven. Master,

Please teach me how to make vows.

Thank you very much.

Answer:

When on one's own, vows can be made with utmost sincerity in front of the Buddhas and Bodhisattvas.

However, vows made under the guidance of a Good Knowing Adviser will be done more correctly, because he or she can advise you as to what kind of vows are appropriate. He or she can then guide you as to how to execute your vows in order to perfect this Paramita.

In general, I would not hesitate to make the vow to find a Good Knowing Adviser from whom to learn Mahayana; it is worth paying any price to find such a teacher. Then I would spare no expense or effort to visit him or her for instruction.

Those who are truly sincere, will definitely be taught.

Buddha Recitation Machine

Question:

Ven. Master:

I practice the Pure Land Dharma Door and have a few questions that I hope you will help clarify for me.

- I leave the Buddha recitation machine on when I go to bed. Is there a difference between the Buddha recitation seeds planted during sleep vs when I am awake?

- I frequently listen to the Buddha recitation machine. Every now and then I have the urge to recite the Buddha's name and then I would hear the recitation sound from the machine. How does that affect my chances of rebirth?

- When I recite the Buddha's name, my mind feels cool and refreshed and I often feel a rush. Is that state actually the Buddha and Bodhisattvas' help as described in the sutras? However, some CDs say that such a state is the result of being touched by yin beings...

Please explain for my sake in order for me to stop worrying and having doubts!

Finally, I wish you health and bliss so that you can quickly realize the Way!

Emituofo

Answer:

Leaving the recitation machine on at night is a good thing. It will continue to plant recitation seeds in your psyche. Of course this is not as effective as listening to the recitation while you are awake, when the recitation seeds have more samadhi power by nature.

The more you recite the Buddha's name, the more rebirth blessings you have.

The key is not necessarily the quantity, but quality, of your recitation. Therefore, when you concentrate more on your recitation, the rebirth blessings are far greater. This is why, when we train our students to cultivate the Pure Land Dharma Door, we stress developing the Buddha recitation samadhi through the proper technique.

Instead of consulting the various resources indiscriminately, you should instead pick and choose the proper Pure Land authorities. I personally would not waste time with materials unless they are from a Buddhist Patriarch.

For example, your CD source regarding the yin beings is totally wrong. I would discard all materials from such a source.

Why Chan and Pure Land Parallel Cultivation?

***Question**:*

Greetings Ven. Master,

I practice Reciting the Buddha's name.

Why do you advocate Chan and Pure Land Parallel Cultivation? Would that not make it difficult to become single-minded?

Emituofo,

***Answer**:*

Good for you!

Several years ago, I started teaching Chan in my living room.

Then a few years later, I decided to teach Chan and Pure Land Parallel Cultivation for these reasons:

1. I realized that most Chan students will not make it through the Chan Dharma Door this lifetime. Therefore I urged them to practice reciting the Buddha's name as an insurance policy.

2. Also, most people who recite the Buddha's name do not know how to attain the Buddha Recitation Samadhi. Their cultivation approach will not bring them to single-mindedness. That was why I urged them to train in our Mahayana Chan methodology as well.

If you feel confident that you can attain single-mindedness through the Buddha Recitation method, stick to it.

However, will you consider this suggestion?

The fact that you even asked me, shows that you do not know how to attain single-mindedness yet. Those who do know would never consider asking me.

Trouble believing in Pure Land Dharma

Question:

Ven. Master:

I find it hard to believe that by merely reciting the Buddha's name, I could obtain rebirth to the Pure Land. My brother said that the Sutras were altered, and that videos about rebirth used professional actors.

Answer:

I do not blame you for being skeptical. Regarding the authenticity of your sources, I too would be skeptical.

Personally, I believe it because my teacher, the late Great Master Xuan Hua said so. He would not lie to me nor has he ever lied to anyone about Buddhism.

Furthermore, I consult the original Buddhist Scriptures known as the Great Treasury Scriptures 大藏經. They are recognized by all Buddhist experts as the indisputable teachings of the Buddha.

After you have planted more blessings with Mahayana, you too will believe.

Aspiring for Rebirth to the Pure Land

***Question**:*

Dear Master YongHua:

I tried meditation. I won't be enlightened doing 30 minutes a day. My mind is full of delusions. The only hope is Other Power of Amitabha and the Bodhisattvas. I want to go to Sukhāvatī, become a bodhisattva and come back to save beings. What do I practice in the morning and night?

Thank you,

W - Brazil

Answer:

Because of its vagueness, this is not a question that can be thoroughly answered in the Q&A section; but I will try.

It seems to me that you have read up on the Pure Land Buddha Dharma.

I advise you to choose your sources carefully. For example, there are naysayers as well as blind devotees whose writings are available on the Internet but they are not credible authorities. You are better off consulting reliable sources such as the Buddhist Patriarchs.

In particular, I would like to recommend literature written by my late master, Great Master Xuan Hua.

Furthermore, I need to caution you on teachers or people who claim that it is easy to attain rebirth to the Pure Land:

experience from teaching these last several years has proved to me otherwise.

In short, you need to get proper information and learn under the guidance of a good teacher. Again, stick to those who are near the main branch of Orthodox Buddhism. This will decrease your chances of going astray, because, like most people, it will be difficult for you to discern right from wrong teachings.

If you are able to, I strongly urge you to come and attend our Buddha recitation week to learn about the Pure Land principles and the proper method of reciting the Buddha's name. This smart initial investment will pay off handsomely down the road.

Best wishes.

Just in Time

[Wife born 1960, had lung cancer for 6 months. Cancer cells proliferated rapidly during these 6 months causing her death. At the time this question was asked, only 2 weeks remained during her 49-day period]

Question:

My wife was a good person. She would not intentionally harm anyone. Why did you say that she is on the way to the animal realm?

Answer:

I apologize for hurting your feelings.

Since you are still very attached to your wife, my straightforward words certainly are of no help.

Follow-up Question:

Didn't you say that she still has another three weeks?

Answer:

Right now, if nothing changes she will most likely be bound for the animal realm. In other words, this is all the current assistance that you have requested can do for her.

That is why we left-home people understand the importance of developing samadhi power to help living beings in critical times like this. The more power we have, the more people we can help and the further we can take them.

Follow-up Question:

Before my wife passed away, my Master came to help. Even though I have been very distraught by my loss, I never stopped reciting the Buddha's name. The past four weeks, my Master and my family have bowed repentances, recited sutras and recited the Buddha's name on her behalf. How come she is still falling to the lower realms?

Answer:

Remember the circumstances of her death. Her cancer went out of control even though she received the best medical care possible.

This shows that her past creditors are very vicious and aim to harm her. They seem to want to send her to the hells, the worst places on earth.

If it weren't for your combined efforts, it could have been worse for her.

Religious Commerce

Question:

The concept of insurance brings to mind the commercial aspects of religion. And we are supposed to buy into the Pure Land scheme?

Agnostic

Answer:

Obviously you have grave doubts that the Pure Land Dharma is true.

Insurance protects you against crippling losses that have a low probability of occurring.

Granted that it is highly likely that you are right and extremely unlikely that you are wrong: this meets the first insurance criteria.

Is it fair to presume that if you lost control of your destiny, and fell to the animal, ghost, or hell realms, this would be personally debilitating? And what if you were mistaken about the Pure Land Dharma Door, which millions of people have already taken advantage of, and which could have helped you as well? Wouldn't this be devastating to your self-esteem?

After you are gone from this world, when you will most likely have to stand before King Yama during the ensuing 49-day period, you will discover that I did not try to cheat you at all. But by then it will be much too late for you and your loved ones.

If you don't understand this lifetime, don't worry. Eventually we will meet again, and then you will believe me. I can be patient: our work spans many lifetimes.

Glossary

12 Conditioned Links: The 12 Conditioned links describe the sequence of causal processes that cause confusion in living beings. This is a Dharma practiced by the Pratyekabuddhas; recall that a Pratyekabuddha is the highest level of attainment in Hinayana Buddhism. By destroying the 12 successive causal links, beginning with the last until they eliminate the first, these great cultivators can eliminate confusion and therefore attain transcendental wisdom.

49-Day Dharma: Buddhists traditionally believe that during this seven-week period right after the time of death, it is crucial to create blessings on behalf of the deceased. These blessings can help the deceased get a better body in their next life or, best yet, attain rebirth to the Pure Land.

Aeon: See kalpa.

Affinity: Affinities are good connections with others. For example, when you give to someone, you create affinity with him and will predispose him to be favorable toward you in the future.

Affliction: An affliction is something that causes us suffering. As far as Buddhism is concerned, anything that stirs up our thinking and gets our mind going is an affliction.

Alaya Consciousness: Often referred to as the soul, and known in Buddhism as the Eighth Consciousness, the Alaya Consciousness carries our karma from one lifetime to the next.

Amitabha Buddha: Amitabha is the Teaching Host of a Buddhaland located far to the West of us. Amitabha Buddha vowed to make it easier for us to escape suffering and attain bliss by bringing us to his Buddhaland, known as the Western Bliss Pure Land. That is why he is often associated with the "Rebirth" or "Pure Land" Dharma Door.

Arhat: The term Arhat is a short designation for a Fourth Stage Arhat, which is a fairly high level of attainment in cultivation. This attainment is associated with the ninth level of samadhi and the ability to bring the thinking mind to a complete stop at will. An Arhat is considered to be one of the two highest levels of attainment in Hinayana Buddhism. The prior levels of attainment to Arhatship are often referred to as First, Second, and Third Stage Arhats.

Attachment: Attachment is the act of holding or keeping something. In Buddhism, it particularly refers to holding onto one's own views and beliefs. Because of attachments, we fail to be open-minded and clear-headed and often don't believe good advice.

Blessings: From the perspective of cause and effect, blessings represent the good karma that we generate by doing good or creating meritorious deeds. For example, help others get what they want and you too will also receive help to get what you want. This is true of blessings in general: they help us get what we want or need. Evil behavior creates absolutely no blessings at all.

Bliss: The indescribably good feeling that arises from entering samadhi, a desired state in meditation, is bliss For example, enter samadhi for 10 minutes and the good feeling may persist for several hours afterwards.

Bodhi: Bodhi is Sanskrit for enlightenment.

Bodhisattva: A Bodhisattva is a superior being who works hard at becoming enlightened. They then work even harder at helping others become enlightened.

Buddhaland: Also known as a world in Buddhism, each Buddhaland has a Buddha who appears in that world and acts as a Teaching Host. Refer to the entry on "world."

Buddha Recitation Samadhi: The Pure Land adherent generally attempts to recite Amitabha Buddha's name 10 times without any intervening thought in between. This is one form of samadhi among the great number of types of samadhis that one can achieve through the various Buddhist practices.

Chan School: One of the Five Schools of Chinese Buddhism, the Chan School focuses on meditation.

Conditioned Links: See 12 Conditioned Links.

Cultivation: This commonly used term refers to the practice of various Buddhist methods. Techniques such as meditation, chanting, bowing, and studying sutras are all forms of cultivation.

Dan Tian: The concept of the *Dan Tian* is borrowed from the Taoists. It is our spiritual center of gravity, physically located around our navel.

Delusion: Also known as inversion, ignorance, stupidity, etc., delusions are erroneous perceptions of the facts. Delusions lead to making wrong choices.

Desire Realm: Humans reside in the Desire Realm, which is the plane of existence characterized by the proliferation of the desires. Because most of us residents of the Desire Realm are unable to concentrate in a sustained way, we are considered to be "scattered."

Dharma: When written with a capital "D," the word Dharma refers to the Buddhadharma: the Buddha's teachings. When written in a lowercase "d", it has very general meaning that literally means 'thing,' and can be applied in various contexts.

Dharma Door: Dharma Door is the technical Buddhist term for an approach or method of practicing the Buddhadharma (or "Dharma"). Buddhism teaches many different Dharma Doors that we can use to break through our barriers and obstructions to enlightenment.

Dharma Master: The Dharma Master is a respectful term that refers to monastics, also known as "left-home people," who speak the Buddhadharma as part of their teaching.

Dharma Realm: The Dharma Realm is a Buddhist term for the entire universe.

Dhyana: The Dhyanas are the beginning states of meditative absorption that are associated with the Form Realm. There are four levels of concentration at this level: the First, Second, Third and Fourth Dhyanas.

Discriminating mind: Also referred to as the conscious mind or the "thinking mind," in non-Buddhist terms, the phrase "discriminating mind" denotes our propensity to make discernments.

Duality: The world as we know it is characterized by duality. Everything exists as pairs of opposites. For instance, when there is love, there also is hate. In addition, these pairs are always changing: new becomes old, cold eventually changes to hot and vice versa.

Expedient: Expedients are sometimes referred to as 'expedient devices,' or 'skill-in-means,' and are practical and pragmatic teaching tools designed to match a student's potential. Wise teachers excel at using temporary expedients to help their pupils understand.

Faith: Faith is the first of the three requisites of the Pure Land practice. One starts by sincerely believing in the teaching.

False-thinking: All mental processing is considered false-thinking because it is performed with the "false" conscious mind.

The Five Schools of Chinese Buddhism: The Five Schools are the Chan, Pure Land, Secret, Precepts, and Study Schools.

Fo Qi: Fo is Chinese for Buddha, Qi is Chinese for seven. This refers to a method of Pure Land practice where the participants get together and recite the Buddha's name for seven days in a row in order to enter the Buddha recitation Samadhi. It is quite effective.

Form Realm: The Form Realm is a plane of existence above the Desire Realm. In addition, the Form Realm refers to a range of concentration levels that can be achieved by cultivating the Four Dhyanas through meditation. The Dhyanas are at times also referred to as the first four levels of samadhi. The beings who live in the Form Realm can easily experience this particular range of concentration levels.

Formless Realm: The Formless Realm is a plane of existence higher than the Form Realm. As with the Form and Desire Realms, the Formless Realm also refers to a respective range of concentration levels that can be achieved by the cultivation of the Fifth through Eighth Samadhis.

Full-lotus: In this meditation posture the legs are crossed by first placing the left foot on top of the right thigh and then the right foot on top of the left thigh.

Gongfu: Gongfu is a Chinese word meaning "skill," and is often applied in the context of martial arts. In this book, gongfu is used interchangeably with samadhi or concentration power.

Good Knowing Adviser: This is a Mahayana term that designates a wise and benevolent teacher.

Guan Yin: Guan Yin is another name for Avalokitesvara Bodhisattva; there is a special Dharma Door that was once practiced by Avalokitesvara Bodhisattva that increases concentration by utilizing our hearing nature. It originates from the Chinese Dharma Door known as "Returning the hearing to listen to one's own nature 反聞聞自性," which is an advanced meditation technique.

Hinayana: Hinayana is a Sanskrit term meaning "Small Vehicle." Vehicle refers to the ability to carry. Small denotes its relatively limited load capacity. Hinayana cultivators focus on their own personal practice, whereas Mahayana, or "Great Vehicle," practitioners develop their wisdom in order to save all living beings.

Hui Yan: This is the name of the Chinese monk credited with founding the Pure Land School of Buddhism in China. He was later recognized as the First Chinese Patriarch of Pure Land Buddhism.

Irreversibility: When one attains the stage of irreversibility in one's practice, one will never again regress on the path toward Buddhahood.

Kalpa: The term "kalpa" denotes a period of time roughly 16 million years in length. One "great kalpa" is equal to 80 kalpas.

Karma: Karma is a Sanskrit term that means "action." There are three types of karmas: those created through our mind, our mouth and our body.

Left-Home Person: This common Buddhist expression refers to monastics who have renounced the "home-life." They have made a vow of celibacy and have given up marriage and family life.

Mahayana: Mahayana is a Sanskrit term for "Big Vehicle." Vehicle refers to the ability to carry or ferry living beings to safety and liberation. Big refers to the much larger load capacity of Mahayana Buddhism, as compared to Hinayana, or "Small Vehicle," Buddhism.

Mantra: Buddhist mantras are special and secret incantations that can command ghosts and spirits. Also known as tantras, these are the mainstay of the Buddhist

Secret School which employs mantras to realize enlightenment.

Medicine Master Buddha: Medicine Master Buddha is the Teaching Host, or current teaching Buddha, of a Buddhaland located far to our East. The Buddhists worship him because it helps them obtain rebirth to his Buddhaland, or to the heavens. Further, by worshiping Medicine Master Buddha, one can also obtain inconceivable benefits while one is alive, such as healing from illnesses, or eradication of disasters, etc. Please refer to our *Medicine Master Buddha Sutra* for more details.

Meddle: Intervening in the natural settlement of past causes and effects is known as meddling. For example, in the natural course of settling past karmic debts, two factions may fight each other. But if a third faction decides to enter into the picture to step in between them and affect the outcome, that is meddling.

Merit and virtue: Whereas one gains merit through visible and observable good actions, one increases one's virtue by improving hidden inner qualities of one's character.

Middle Way: The Middle Way is another name for Buddhism. The Middle Way is differentiated from the practices of extreme indulgence, advocated by the "Permanence camp," or extreme mortification, advocated by the "Nihilism camp." The Buddha accomplished his practice by renouncing those two extreme practices, instead applying moderation in his cultivation.

Mindfulness: Mindfulness is a concept that has gained popularity in recent years, and has several related meanings. To be mindful is to keep something in mind and not forget it. Mahayana Pure Land Buddhism teaches the method of being mindful of Amitabha Buddha's name, in which one recites his name to the point where one is no longer interrupted by false-thinking.

Nature: Also known as one's Self-Nature, this refers to the Buddha Nature that we all already possess. To "see the Nature" is to see the truth and thus end one's delusions.

Nirvana: A plane of existence characterized as "Unproduced" or "Unborn" and "Unextinguished" or "Non-dying." To "enter Nirvana" is very desirable because in that state, you are your true self, totally pure (undefiled) and free from suffering. You experience only permanent bliss. In other words, you have escaped the Wheel of Reincarnation.

Noumena: Noumena refers to the principles of Buddhism, and is contrasted with phenomenon, which refers to the instances or manifestations of those principles.

One Mind Unconfused: This is another term for the Buddha Recitation samadhi.

Outflows: The concept of an outflow refers to our inability to stop our mind from chasing outside ourselves, which causes our wisdom life to diminish. For instance, when our sense organs contact the world, our energy leaks out, which is clearly undesirable.

Paramita: Paramita is Sanskrit for "arriving at the other shore" or "successful completion." The Bodhisattvas practice the Six Paramitas as part of their cultivation to become enlightened.

The Patience of Non-production of Dharmas: This is the official designation of the Ninth Samadhi. When one reaches the Patience of Non-production of Dharmas, not a single thought is generated: that is true self-control.

Patriarch: Mahayana patriarchs are enlightened beings who are recognized for their commitment to propagating a particular school of Buddhist teachings.

Phenomenon: Phenomenon refers to the examples or manifestations of an underlying principle, which is often referred to in Buddhism as noumenon. For example, a noumenon could be the law of cause and effect. One corresponding phenomenon could be experiencing pleasurable results due to good karma one created in the past.

Practice: In the context of the Pure Land Dharma, the term 'Practice' usually refers to the third of the three requisites for the successful cultivation of the Pure Land Dharma Door. After making vows to obtain rebirth to the Pure Lands, we should take action in order to make it happen: we must practice. That is why many Pure Land adherents fervently recite Amitabha Buddha's name, hoping to enter the Buddha Recitation Samadhi, so that they can attain rebirth to his Pure Land.

Pratyekabuddha: A Pratyekabuddha is a sage in the Hinayana tradition. Like Arhats, they are also able to stop their discursive thoughts. However, Pratyekabuddhas have a higher level of transcendental wisdom than that of an Arhat. They reach this level of attainment by practicing the Dharma Door of the 12 Conditioned Links.

Precepts: The Buddhist rules of morality are known as the precepts.

Precepts School: One of the Five Schools of Chinese Buddhism, this school emphasizes careful study and practice of the precepts, or Vinaya.

Pure Land: The phrase "Pure Land" is typically used as an abbreviation for the Western Bliss Pure Land of Amitabha Buddha. However, there are in fact many other Pure Lands as well. These Pure Lands can be considered the Buddhist heavens, if you will.

Pure Land School: Of the Five Schools of Chinese Buddhism, the Pure Land School is the most widely practiced.

Rebirth: This term generally refers to the Buddhist belief that after death we will be reborn into another body, but in many contexts, "rebirth" is often used by the Pure Land adherents as short for "rebirth to the Pure Land."

Rebirth Grade: This refers to the level of social status in Amitabha Buddha's Pure Land. There are nine major grades. The topmost is the ninth grade, which is usually the rebirth grade for advanced practitioners such as the Bodhisattvas.

Saha World: The Saha World is the world we live in. However, in Buddhism our Saha World is regarded as being much larger than just a single planet. In fact the Saha World corresponds to the entire Milky Way galaxy. Shakyamuni Buddha is the Teaching Host of the Saha World.

Samadhi: Generally, the Sanskrit word samadhi denotes the ability to enter concentrative states; more specifically, samadhi refers to concentration levels ranging from the

Four Dhyanas of the Form Realm to the Four Stations of the Formless Realm.

Secret School: One of the five major schools of Chinese Buddhism, the Secret School advocates the practice of reciting mantras.

Self: The small self is just our selfish and petty self; the Big Self is the Buddha Nature.

Single-mindedness: Single-mindedness is the ability to focus on one thought to the exclusion of all other thoughts.

Store: This is a general designation of the three classes of Buddhist teachings, which are: 1) The Sutra Store, for the study of samadhi; 2) The Vinaya Store, for the study of the rules of morality; and 3) the Shastra Store, for the study of transcendental wisdom.

Study School: One of the Five Schools of Chinese Buddhism, the Study School focuses on studying the Sutras.

Suffering: Since in the past we created offenses, or bad karma, we must now bear the consequences and undergo suffering, which can be physical, mental, or emotional.

Sutra: Sutra is a general term that designates the teachings of the Buddha. Buddhists study sutras in order to understand how to cultivate samadhi.

Tantra: Same meaning as mantra.

Ten Thousand: This phrase originates from the Chinese culture and denotes a large number.

Three Evil Paths: The Three Evil Paths, which are also known as the three evil destinies, refer to the hells, the hungry ghost realm and the animal realm. When one creates karma by way of the three poisons, one creates the causes to fall to the three evil destinies upon death.

Three Poisons: The Three Poisons are greed, anger and stupidity. These three character flaws poison us and defile our Buddha Nature.

Transcendental: We cultivate in order to learn how to transcend the Triple Realm. Those who have accomplished this are said to have transcendental wisdom.

Triple Jewel: Also known as the Three Gems, the Triple Jewel consists of: 1) The Buddha Jewel – all the Buddhas in the universe, 2) the Dharma Jewel – the teachings of all Buddhas, and 3) the Sangha Jewel – the left-home people.

Triple Realm: Often referred to as samsara, the Triple Realm consists of the Desire, Form and Formless Realms, which living beings cycle through in the "wheel of reincarnation." We practice in order to escape from this incessant transmigration.

True Nature: This refers to the Buddha Nature inherent in all living beings, and is often simply referred as our "Nature."

True Suchness: True Suchness is another term for the Buddha's state of Nirvana.

Vajra: Vajra is the name of the hardest substance in the universe. It cannot be mined but must be cultivated with the Buddhadharma.

Vow: Making vows is the second of the three requisites of the Pure Land practice. One resolves to attain rebirth to the Pure Land because the Buddhas and Bodhisattvas would never force their will upon the faithful.

Western Bliss Pure Land: This is the full name of the Pure Land where Amitabha Buddha is currently teaching. The Sanskrit name for Amitabha's Pure Land is Sukhāvatī, known in Chinese as *Jílè* 極樂 ("Ultimate Bliss"), *Ānlè* 安樂 ("Peaceful Bliss"), or *Xītiān* 西天 ("Western Heaven"). This is by far the easiest Pure Land to which the inhabitants of our world can attain rebirth.

World: In Buddhist language, a world refers to an entire world system, which corresponds to a galaxy, in contemporary understanding.

Amitabha Buddha

Dharma Master YongHua

Master YongHua's Biography

A native of Vietnam, Dharma Master YongHua came to the United States for college where he earned a Bachelor of Science and a Master of Business Administration, with the aspiration of eventually returning to Vietnam to help rebuild his war-ravaged country. However, after climbing up the corporate ladder and reaching executive management positions, he found himself disillusioned with the business world. Around this time, he was exposed to Great Master Xuan Hua's teachings, which inspired him to enter monastic training. He soon realized that he had discovered his true calling, and decided to dedicate the rest of his life to serving Buddhism.

Master YongHua not only studied meditation in the Gui Yang Lineage of Great Master Xuan Hua, but also inherited the Lin Ji lineage from Master Man Giac. Now that he has investigated Mahayana for more than 20 years, Master YongHua continues the Buddhist tradition of "repaying his teachers' kindness" by extensively speaking on the Buddhadharma and vigorously training the next generation of cultivators. In the past several years, many of Master YongHua's students have become accomplished meditators and Pure Land practitioners.

Master YongHua advocates the parallel practice of Chan and Pure Land. This way those who have the potential can obtain immediate liberation through Chan. Furthermore, at the end of this lifetime, all those who truly believe will have the chance for rebirth to the Pure Land. Master YongHua offers a practical, contemporary explanation of the Buddha's ancient teachings in order to help us penetrate the sages' wisdom and apply it to our daily lives, hoping that all living beings will quickly escape suffering and attain bliss.

Printed in Great Britain
by Amazon